The Industrial Revolution and Free Trade

Edited by Burton W. Folsom, Jr.

Foundation for Economic Education
Irvington-on-Hudson, NY 10533

The Industrial Revolution and Free Trade

The Foundation for Economic Education, Inc.
30 South Broadway
Irvington-on-Hudson, NY 10533
(914) 591-7230

Publisher's Cataloging in Publication
(Prepared by Quality Books Inc.)

The industrial revolution and free trade / edited by Burton W. Folsom, Jr.
    p. cm.
    ISBN: 1-57246-057-1
    Includes index.

    1. Free trade. 2. Industrial revolution. 3. Capitalism. 4. Commerce. I. Folsom, Burton W.

HF1713.I64 1996   382'.71
                   QBI96-40665

Library of Congress Catalog Card Number: 96-061674

Cover design by Beth R. Bowlby
Manufactured in the United States of America

Table of Contents

Introduction

In 1764, James Hargreaves, an uneducated weaver from Lancashire, England, displayed a remarkable invention. It was a hand-cranked machine that could spin yarn on eight spindles. He called his contraption a "spinning jenny"; later models of Hargreaves' jenny had up to 120 spindles. The replacement of hand-spinning by machine was one of several inventions that mechanized the making of clothes, which allowed a factory of specialized workers to make in a day what once took a year. The Industrial Revolution was born.

The Industrial Revolution, with its mass production in factories, transformed first England and then the world. As textile mills soaked up capital, farmers were drawn to growing cities to take jobs in the factories. The era of the specialist had begun: cotton producers, weavers, builders, loom repairmen, dyemakers, cutters, wholesalers, retailers, and marketing experts all made the British textile industry a driving force in the world. This specialized labor, this disciplined work force, this competition for markets would later be repeated in the iron and steel industry. British entrepreneurs went from making pins and nails to plows and rails. During the 1800s, they tied the world together with steamships, railroads, telegraphs, and telephones.

What would be the relationship between the Industrial Revolution and free trade? What would be the balance between liberty and authority in this new industrial society? At first, the answers to these questions were not clear. The political economy of the 1700s was dominated by the idea of mercantilism—which urged nations to be self-sufficient, to shun imports and promote exports, and to build their supplies of gold. Therefore, the European mercantilist empires of the 1700s were highly restrictive: tariffs, subsidies, monopolies, and government contracts abounded.

Even as Hargreaves was inventing and perfecting his spinning jenny, however, the ideas of free trade and private enterprise were finding their way into print. William Blackstone, in the 1760s, published his *Commentaries on the Laws of England*. According to Blackstone:

> The absolute rights of man, considered as a free agent, endowed with discernment to know good from evil, and with power of choosing those measures which appear to him to be most desirable, are usually summed up in one general appella-

1

tion and denominated the natural liberty of mankind. This natural liberty consists properly in a power of acting as one thinks fit, without any restraint or control, unless by the law of nature; being a right inherent in us by birth, and one of the gifts of God to man at his creation, when he endued him with the faculty of free will.

When Adam Smith wrote *The Wealth of Nations* in 1776, he applied this idea of natural liberty to the nation state:

What is prudence in the conduct of every private family, can scarce be folly in that of a great kingdom. If a foreign country can supply us with a commodity cheaper than we ourselves can make it, better buy it of them. . . . In every country, it always is and must be the interest of the great body of the people to buy whatever they want of those who sell it cheapest. The proposition is so very manifest, that it seems ridiculous to take any pains to prove it; nor could it ever have been called in question, had not the interested sophistry of merchants and manufacturers confounded the common sense of mankind. Their interest is, in this respect, directly opposite to that of the great body of the people.

In this "system of natural liberty," Smith argued, an invisible hand in the marketplace helped transform mere private gains into public usefulness:

It is not from the benevolence of the butcher, the brewer, or the baker, that we expect our dinner, but from their regard to their own interest. We address ourselves, not to their humanity but to their self-love, and never talk to them of our own necessities but of their advantages.

In 1850, Richard Cobden, the British political leader, argued further that "free trade would have a tendency to unite mankind in the bonds of peace."

If free trade was moral, if it was efficient, if it promoted liberty and public progress, and if it promoted international peace, then what was the proper role of government in this new society. "According to the system of natural liberty," Adam Smith argued:

the sovereign has only three duties to attend to; three duties of great importance, indeed, but plain and intelligible to common understandings: first, the duty of protecting the society from the violence and invasion of other independent societies; secondly, the duty of protecting, as far as possible, every member of society from the justice or oppression of every other member of it, or the duty of establishing an exact administration of justice; and thirdly, the duty of erecting and maintaining certain public works and certain public institutions, which it can never be for the interest of any individual, or small number of individuals, to erect and maintain; because the profit could never repay the expense to any individual or small number of individuals, though it may frequently do much more than repay it to a great society.

Smith's case for free trade and limited government won the battle of ideas in the 1800s. The Industrial Revolution and the free trade that followed brought rising standards of living to many Western countries. Those countries outside the Western orbit watched the rise of industrialism with different attitudes. The Chinese, for example, remained isolationist. They limited their trade with the West and refused to adopt new technology or new ideas about individual liberty.

In 1793, Ch'ien Lung, the Chinese emperor, wrote a classic letter to George III of England. King George, it seems, wanted more trade with China and sent a batch of British goods there to excite curiosity and open doors for future trade. Ch'ien Lung dismissed Britain's "precious objects." "There is nothing we lack," he smugly wrote. "We have never set much store on strange or ingenious objects, nor do we need any more of your country's manufactures. . . ." In the 1800s, China followed Ch'ien Lung's policy whenever possible. While Western countries built factories, railroads, and military equipment, China retreated into its shell.

Japan's attitude was completely different. From the moment Commodore Matthew Perry opened up Japan for trade in 1854, the Japanese began to copy Western technology. The Meiji dynasty encouraged textile production and Japan soon challenged the West in the making of clothes. Ships, railroads, and guns would soon follow. In 1871, novelist Kanagaki Robun captured popular sentiment in Japan toward the West when he wrote, "In the West they're free of superstitions. There it's the custom to do everything scientifically, and that's why they've invented amazing things like the steamship and the steam engine. . . . Aren't they wonderful inventions?"

To compare the views of Ch'ien Lung and Kanagaki Robun on trade is to understand the history of China and Japan in the 1800s. In the 1840s and 1850s, China lost wealth and land (including Hong Kong) to England and France during the Opium Wars. Later in the century, the European powers carved the hapless Chinese nation into spheres of influence. Japan by contrast, industrialized so quickly that it soon rivaled the leading Western countries. In 1895, Japan crushed China in a major war; ten years later Japan took on the Russians and thrashed them convincingly.

The nineteenth-century examples of England, China, and Japan, then, gave the world a tentative history lesson: Those nations that industrialize and open themselves to trade will advance financially and militarily. What the twentieth century has provided, however, is an ironic twist of this lesson. The Western nations, which had led the world in individual liberty, seemed more and more threatened by free trade. The United States, for example, at the peak of its industrial hegemony during the 1920s, decided to erect high tariff barriers. When the Great Depression took hold after 1929, the United States responded by pushing the tariffs even higher. The Smoot-Hawley Tariff, passed in 1930, taxed 3,218 items; over one-fourth of these were sharply increased under Smoot-Hawley. The result was increased disaster and stagnation for all Western nations. When the United States, for example, tariffed Swiss watches, the Swiss retaliated and tariffed American cars, vacuum cleaners, and typewriters.

The non-Western nations, by contrast, even the dictatorships, sometimes used trade to catch up with the West. The Russians, for example, under Lenin and Stalin, appropriated grain from millions of peasants and sent it to Europe in exchange for mining, railroad, telegraph, and sawmill technology. These trade advantages gained by the Russians were, of course, largely negated by the stifling controls they imposed on local entrepreneurs and the local economy. As the twentieth century comes to an end, however, the non-Western countries of Hong Kong, Taiwan, and Singapore are flourishing by doing what the Western powers did a century ago—industrialize, encourage entrepreneurs, and trade freely.

—BURTON W. FOLSOM, JR.
Senior Fellow in Economic Education
Mackinac Center for Public Policy
Midland, Michigan

September 1996

I. THEORIES AND THEORISTS

Mercantilism: A Lesson for Our Times?

by Murray N. Rothbard

Mercantilism has had a "good press" during much of the twentieth century. In the days of Adam Smith and the classical economists, by contrast, mercantilism was properly regarded as a blend of economic fallacy and state creation of special privilege. But in our century, the general view of mercantilism has changed drastically: Keynesians hail mercantilists as prefiguring their own economic insights; Marxists, constitutionally unable to distinguish between free enterprise and special privilege, hail mercantilism as a "progressive" step in the historical development of capitalism; socialists and interventionists salute mercantilism as anticipating modern state-building and central planning.

Mercantilism, which reached its height in the Europe of the seventeenth and eighteenth centuries, was a system of statism which employed economic fallacy to build up a structure of imperial state power, as well as special subsidy and monopolistic privilege to individuals or groups favored by the state. Thus, mercantilism held that exports should be encouraged by the government and imports discouraged. Economically, this seems to be a tissue of fallacy; for what is the point of exports if not to purchase imports, and what is the point of piling up gold if the gold is not used to purchase goods?

But mercantilism cannot be viewed satisfactorily as merely an exercise in economic theory. The mercantilist writers, indeed, did not consider themselves economic theorists, but practical men of affairs who argued and pamphleteered for specific economic policies, generally for policies which would subsidize activities or companies in which those writers were interested. Thus, a policy of favoring exports and penalizing imports had two important practical effects: it subsidized merchants and manufacturers engaged in the export trade, and it threw up a wall of privilege around inefficient manufacturers who formerly had to compete with foreign rivals. At the same time, the network of regu-

Dr. Rothbard (1926–1995) was the S.J. Hall Distinguished Professor of Economics at the University of Nevada, Las Vegas, and Academic Vice President of the Ludwig von Mises Institute. Among his works are the comprehensive treatise *Man, Economy, and State* (1962) and *America's Great Depression* (1963). This article was originally published in the November 1963 issue of *The Freeman*.

lation and its enforcement built up the state bureaucracy as well as national and imperial power.

The famous English Navigation Acts, which played a leading role in provoking the American Revolution, are an excellent example of the structure and purpose of mercantilist regulation. The network of restriction greatly penalized Dutch and other European shippers, as well as American shipping and manufacturing, for the benefit of English merchants and manufacturers, whose competition was either outlawed or severely taxed and crippled. The use of the state to cripple or prohibit one's competition is, in effect, the grant by the state of monopolistic privilege; and such was the effect for Englishmen engaged in the colonial trade.

A further consequence was the increase of tax revenue to build up the power and wealth of the English government, as well as the multiplying of the royal bureaucracy needed to administer and enforce the regulations and tax decrees. Thus, the English government, and certain English merchants and manufacturers, benefited from these mercantilist laws; the losers included foreign merchants, American merchants and manufacturers, and, above all, the *consumers* of all lands, including England itself. The consumers lost, not only because of the specific distortions and restrictions on production of the various decrees, but also from the hampering of the international division of labor imposed by all the regulations.

Adam Smith's Refutation

Mercantilism, then, was not simply an embodiment of theoretical fallacies; for the laws were *only* fallacious if we look at them from the point of view of the consumer, or of each individual in society. They are not fallacious if we realize that their aim was to confer special privilege and subsidy on favored groups. Since subsidy and privilege can only be conferred by government *at the expense* of the remainder of its citizens. The fact that the bulk of the consumers lost in the process should occasion little surprise.[1]

Contrary to general opinion, the classical economists were not content merely to refute the fallacious economics of such mercantilist theories as bullionism or protectionism; they also were perfectly aware of the drive for special privilege that propelled the "mercantile system." Thus, Adam Smith pointed to the fact that linen yarn could be imported into England duty free, whereas heavy import duties were levied on finished woven linen. The reason, as seen by Smith, was that the numerous English yarn-spinners did not constitute a strong pressure-group, whereas the master-weavers were able to pressure the government to impose high duties on their product, while making sure that their raw material could be bought at as low a price as possible. He concluded that the

> motive of all these regulations, is to extend our own manufactures, not by their own improvement, but by the depression of those of all our neighbors, and by putting an end, as much as possible, to the troublesome competition of such odious and disagreeable rivals. . . .
>
> Consumption is the sole end and purpose of all production; and the interest of the producer ought to be attended to, only so far as it may be necessary for promoting that of the consumer. . . . But in the mercantile system, the interest of the consumer is almost constantly sacrificed to that of the producer; and it seems to consider production, and not consumption, as the ultimate end and object of all industry and commerce.
>
> In the restraints upon the importation of all foreign commodities which can come into competition with those of our own growth, or manufacture, the interest of the home-consumer is evidently sacrificed to that of the producer. It is altogether for the benefit of the latter, that the former is obliged to pay that enhancement of price which this monopoly almost always occasions.
>
> It is altogether for the benefit of the producer that bounties are granted upon the exportation of some of his productions. The home-consumer is obliged to pay, first, the tax which is necessary for paying the bounty, and secondly, the still greater tax which necessarily arises from enhancement of the price of the commodity in the home market.[2]

Before Keynes

Mercantilism was not only a policy of intricate government regulations; it was also a pre-Keynesian policy of inflation, of lowering interest rates artificially, and of increasing "effective demand" by heavy government spending and sponsorship of measures to increase the quantity of money. Like the Keynesians, the mercantilists thundered against "hoarding," and urged the rapid circulation of money throughout the economy; furthermore, they habitually pointed to an alleged "scarcity of money" as the cause of depressed trade or unemployment.[3] Thus, in a prefiguration of the Keynesian "multiplier," William Potter, one of the first advocates of paper money in the Western world (1650), wrote:

> The greater quantity . . . of money . . . the more commodity they sell, that is, the greater is their trade. For whatsoever is taken amongst men . . . though it were ten times more than now it is, yet if it be one way or other laid out by each man, as fast as he receives it . . . it doth occasion a quickness in the revolution of commodity from hand to hand . . . much more than proportional to such increase of money. . . .[4]

And the German mercantilist F. W. von Schrötter wrote of the importance of money changing hands, for one person's spending is another's income; as money "pass[es] from one hand to another . . . the more useful it is to the country, for . . . the sustenance of so many people is multiplied," and employment increased. Thrift, according to von Schrötter, causes unemployment, since saving withdraws money from circulation. And John Cary wrote that if everyone spent more, everyone would obtain larger incomes, and "might then live more plentifully."[5]

Historians have had an unfortunate tendency to depict the mercantilists as inflationists and *therefore* as champions of the poor debtors, while the classical economists have been considered hard-hearted apologists for the *status quo* and the established order. The truth was almost precisely the reverse. In the first place, inflation did not benefit the poor; wages habitually lagged behind the rise in prices during inflations, especially behind agricultural prices. Furthermore, the "debtors" were generally not the poor but large merchants and quasi-feudal landlords, and it was the landlords who benefited triply from inflation: from the habitually steep increases in food prices, from the lower interest rates and the lower purchasing-power of money in their role as debtors, and from the particularly large increases in land values caused by the fall in interest rates. In fact, the English government and Parliament was heavily landlord-dominated, and it is no coincidence that one of the main arguments of the mercantilist writers for inflation was that it would greatly raise the value of land.

Exploitation of Workers

Far from being true friends of laborers, the mercantilists were frankly interested in exploiting their labor to the utmost; full employment was urged as a means of maximizing such exploitation. Thus, the mercantilist William Petyt wrote frankly of labor as "capital material

. . . raw and undigested . . . committed into the hands of supreme authority, in whose prudence and disposition it is to improve, manage, and fashion it to more or less advantage."[6] Professor Furniss comments that "it is characteristic of these writers that they should be so readily disposed to trust in the wisdom of the civil power to 'improve, manage, and fashion' the economic 'raw material' of the nation. Bred of this confidence in statecraft, proposals were multiplied for exploiting the labor of the people as the chief source of national wealth, urging upon the rulers of the nation divers[e] schemes for directing and creating employment. . . ."[7] The mercantilist's attitude toward labor and full employment is also indicated by his dislike of holidays, by which the "nation" was deprived of certain amounts of labor; the desire of the individual worker for leisure was never considered worthy of note.

Compulsory Employment

The mercantilist writers realized frankly that the corollary to a guarantee of full employment is coerced labor for those who don't wish to work or to work in the employment desired by the guarantors. One writer summed up the typical view: "It is absolutely necessary that employment should be provided for persons of every age that are able and willing to work, and the idle and refractory should be sent to the house of correction, there to be detained and constantly kept to labor." Henry Fielding wrote that "the constitution of a society in this country having a claim on all its members, has a right to insist on the labor of the poor as the only service they can render." And George Berkeley asked rhetorically "whether temporary servitude would not be the best cure for idleness and beggary? . . . Whether sturdy beggars may not be seized and made slaves to the public for a certain term of years?"[8] William Temple proposed a scheme to send the children of laborers, from the age of four on, to public workhouses, where they would be kept "fully employed" for at least twelve hours a day," for by these means we hope that the rising generation will be habituated to constant employment. . . ." And another writer expressed his amazement that parents tended to balk at these programs:

> Parents . . . from whom to take for time the idle, mischievous, least useful and most burdensome part of their family to bring them up without any care or expense to themselves in habits of industry and decency is a very great relief; are very much adverse to sending their children . . . from what cause, it is difficult to tell.[9]

Perhaps the most misleading legend about the classical economists is that they were apologists for the *status quo*; on the contrary, they were "radical" libertarian opponents of the established Tory mercantilist order of big government, restrictionism, and special privilege. Thus, Professor Fetter writes that during the first half of the nineteenth century, the

> *Quarterly Review* and *Blackwood's Edinburgh Magazine*, staunch supporters of the established order, and opponents of change in virtually all fields, had no sympathy with political economy or with laissez-faire, and were constantly urging maintenance of tariffs, expenditures by government, and suspension of the gold standard in order to stimulate demand and increase employment. On the other hand the *Westminster's* [journal of the classical liberals] support of the gold standard and free trade, and its opposition to any attempt to stimulate the economy by positive government action, came not from believers in authority or from defenders of the dominant social force behind authority, but from the most articulate intellectual radicals of the time and the severest critics of the established order.[10]

Southey Favors Nationalization

In contrast, let us consider the *Quarterly Review*, a high Tory journal which always "assumed that the unreformed Parliament, the dominance of a landed aristocracy . . . the supremacy of the established church, discrimination of some sort against Dissenter, Catholic, and Jew, and the keeping of the lower classes in their place were the foundations of a stable society." Their leading writer on economic problems, the poet Robert Southey, repeatedly urged government expenditure as a stimulant to economic activity, and attacked England's resumption of specie payments (return to the gold standard) after the Napoleonic Wars. Indeed, Southey proclaimed that an increase in taxes or in the public debt was never a cause for alarm, since they "give a spur to the national industry, and call forth national energies." And, in 1816, Southey advocated a large public works program for relief of unemployment and depression.[11]

The *Quarterly Review's* desire for stringent government control and even ownership of the railroads was at least frankly linked with its hatred of the benefits that railroads were bringing to the mass of the British population. Thus, where the classical liberals hailed the advent of railroads as bringing cheaper transportation and as thereby increasing the mobility of labor, the *Quarterly*'s John Croker denounced railroads as "rendering travel too cheap and easy— unsettling the habits of the poor, and tempting them to improvident migration."[12]

The arch-Tory William Robinson, who often denounced his fellow Tories for compromising even slightly on such principles as high tariffs and no political rights for Catholics, wrote many pre-Keynesian articles, advocating inflation to stimulate production and employment, and denouncing the hard-money effects of the gold standard. And Sir Archibald Alison, a Tory and an inveterate advocate of inflation who even ascribed the fall of the Roman Empire to a shortage of money, frankly admitted that it was the agricultural class that had suffered from the lack of inflation since resumption of the gold standard.[13]

Controls Under Elizabeth

A few case studies will illustrate the nature of mercantilism, the reasons for mercantilist decrees, and some of the consequences that they brought to the economy.

One important part of mercantilist policy was wage controls. In the fourteenth century, the Black Death killed one-third of the laboring population of England, and naturally brought sharp advances in wage rates. Wage controls came in as wage-ceilings, in desperate attempts by the ruling classes to coerce wage rates below their market price. And since the vast bulk of employed laborers were agricultural workers, this was clearly legislation for the benefit of the feudal landlords and to the detriment of the workers.

Textiles vs. Agriculture

The result was a persistent shortage of agricultural and other unskilled laborers for centuries, a shortage mitigated by the fact that the English government did not try to enforce the laws very rigorously. When Queen Elizabeth tried to enforce the wage controls strictly, the agricultural labor shortage was aggravated, and the landlords found their statutory privileges defeated by the more subtle laws of the market. Consequently, Elizabeth passed, in 1563, the famous Statute of Artificers, imposing comprehensive labor control.

Attempting to circumvent the shortage caused by previous interventions, the statute installed forced labor on the land. It provided that: (1) whoever had worked on the land until the age of 12 be compelled to remain there and not leave for work at any other trade; (2) all craftsmen, servants, and apprentices who had no great reputation in their fields be forced to harvest wheat; and (3) unemployed persons be compelled to work as agricultural laborers. In addition, the statute prohibited any worker from quitting his job unless he had a license proving that he had already been hired by another employer. And, furthermore, justices of the peace were ordered to set maximum wage rates, geared to changes in the cost of living.

The statute also acted to restrict the growth of the woolen textile industry; this benefited two groups: the landlords, who would no longer lose laborers to industry and suffer the pressure of paying higher wage rates, and the textile industry itself, which received the privilege of keeping out the competition of new firms or new craftsmen. The coerced immobility of labor, however, led to suffering for all workers, including textile craftsmen; and to remedy the latter, Queen Elizabeth imposed a minimum wage law for textile craftsmen, thundering all the while that the wicked clothing manufacturers were responsible for the craftsmen's plight. Fortunately, textile employers and workers persisted in agreeing on terms of employment below the artificially set wage rate, and heavy textile unemployment did not yet arise.

Enforcing Bad Laws

The program of wage controls could not cause undue dislocations until they were stringently enforced, and this came to pass under King James I, the first Stuart king of England. Upon assuming the throne in 1603, James decided to enforce the Elizabethan control program with great stringency, including extremely heavy penalties against employers. Rigorous enforcement was imposed on minimum wage controls for textile craftsmen, and on maximum wage decrees for agricultural laborers and servants.

The consequences were the inevitable result of tampering with the laws of the market: chronic severe unemployment throughout the textile industry, coupled with a chronic severe shortage of agricultural labor. Misery and discontent spread throughout the land. Citizens were fined for paying their servants more than ceiling wages, and servants fined for accepting the pay. James, and his son Charles I, decided to stem the tide of unemployment in textiles by compelling employers to remain in business even when they were losing money. But even though many employers were jailed for infractions, such Draconian measures could not keep the textile industry from depression, stagnation, and unemployment. Certainly the consequences of the policy of wage controls was one of the reasons for the overthrow of the Stuarts' monarchy in the mid-seventeenth century.

Mercantilist Practices in Colonial Massachusetts

The young colony of Massachusetts engaged in a great many mercantilist ventures, with invariably unfortunate results. One attempt was a comprehensive program of wage and price controls, which had to be abandoned by the 1640s. Another was a series of subsidies to try to create industries in the colony before they were economically viable, and therefore before they would be created on the free market. One example was iron manufacture. Early iron mines in America were small and located in coastal swamps ("bog iron"), and primary manufactured, or "wrought," iron was made cheaply in local bloomeries, at an open hearth. The Massachusetts government decided, however, to force the creation of the more imposing—and far more expensive—indirect process of wrought iron manufacture at a blast furnace and forge. The Massachusetts legislature therefore decreed that any new iron mine must have a furnace and forge constructed near it within ten years of its discovery. Not content with this measure, the legislature in 1645 granted a new Company of Undertakers For An Iron Works In New England, a 21-year monopoly of all ironmaking in the colony. In addition, the legislature granted the company generous subsidies of timber land.

But despite these subsidies and privileges, as well as additional large grants of timberland from the town governments of Boston and Dorchester, the Company's venture failed dismally and almost immediately. The Company did its best to salvage its operations, but to no avail. A few years later, John Winthrop, Jr., the main promoter of the older venture, induced the authorities of New Haven colony to subsidize an iron manufacture of his at Stony River. From the governments of New Haven colony and New Haven township, Winthrop was granted a whole host of special subsidies: land grants, payment of all costs of building the furnace, a dam on the river, and the transportation of fuel. One of Winthrop's partners in the venture was the deputy-governor of the colony, Stephen Goodyear, who was thus able to use the power of government to grant himself substantial privileges. But again, economic law was not to be denied, and the ironworks proved to be another rapidly failing concern.

Debtors' Relief: A Scheme to Aid the Rich

One of the most vigorously held tenets of the dominant neo-Marx-ist historians of America has been the view that inflation and debtors' relief were always measures of the "lower classes," the poor farmer-debtors and sometimes urban workers, engaging in a Marxian class struggle against conservative merchant-creditors. But a glance at the origins of debtors' relief and paper money in America easily shows the fallacy of this approach; inflation and debtors' relief were mercantilist measures, pursued for familiar mercantilist ends.

Debtors' relief began in the colonies, in Massachusetts in 1640. Massachusetts had experienced a sharp economic crisis in 1640, and the debtors turned immediately to special privilege from the government. Obediently, the legislature of Massachusetts passed the first of a series of debtors' relief laws in October, including a minimum-appraisal law to force creditors to accept insolvent debtors' property at an arbitrarily inflated assessment, and a legal-tender provision to compel creditors to accept payment in an inflated, fixed rate in the monetary media of the day: corn, cattle, or fish.

Further privileges to debtors were passed in 1642 and 1644, the latter permitting a debtor to escape foreclosure simply by leaving the colony. The most drastic proposal went to the amazing length of providing that the Massachusetts government assume all private debts that could not be paid! This plan was passed by the upper house, but defeated in the house of deputies.

The fact that this astounding bill was passed by the *upper* house—the council of magistrates—is evidence enough that this was not a proto-Marxian eruption of poor debtors. For this council was the ruling group of the colony, consisting of the wealthiest merchants and landowners. If not for historical myths, it should occasion no surprise that the biggest debtors were the wealthiest men of the colony, and that in the mercantilist era a drive for special privilege should have had typically mercantilist aims. On the other hand, it is also instructive that the more democratic and popularly responsible lower house was the one far more resistant to the debt relief program.

Paper Money Inflation

Massachusetts has the dubious distinction of having promulgated the first governmental paper money in the history of the Western world—indeed, in the history of the entire world outside of China. The fateful issue was made in 1690, to pay for a plunder expedition against

French Canada that had failed drastically. But even before this, the leading men of the colony were busy proposing paper money schemes. The Reverend John Woodbridge, greatly influenced by William Potter's proposals for an inflationary land bank, proposed one of his own, as did Governor John Winthrop, Jr., of Connecticut. Captain John Blackwell proposed a land bank in 1686, the notes of which would be legal tender in the colony, and such wealthy leaders of the colony as Joseph Dudley, William Stoughton, and Wait Winthrop were prominently associated with the plan.

The most famous of the inflationary land-bank schemes was the Massachusetts Land Bank of 1740, which has generally been limned in neo-Marxist terms as the creation of the mass of poor farmer-debtors over the opposition of wealthy merchant-creditors of Boston. In actuality, its founder, John Colman, was a prominent Boston merchant and real-estate speculator; and its other supporters had similar interests—*as did* the leading opponents, who were also Boston businessmen. The difference is that the advocates had generally been receivers of land grants from the Massachusetts government, and desired inflation to raise the value of their speculatively held land claims.[14] Once again—this was a typically mercantilist project.

Keynes Wouldn't Learn

From just a brief excursion into mercantilist theory and practice, we may conclude that Lord Keynes might have come to regret his enthusiastic welcome to the mercantilists as his forbears. For they were his forbears indeed; and the precursors as well of the interventions, subsidies, regulations, grants of special privilege, and central planning of today. But in no way could they be considered as "progressives" or lovers of the common man; on the contrary, they were frank exponents of the old order of statism, hierarchy, landed oligarchy, and special privilege— that entire "Tory" regime against which laissez-faire liberalism and classical economics leveled their liberating "revolution" on behalf of the freedom and prosperity of *all* productive individuals in society, from the wealthiest to the humblest. Perhaps the modern world will learn the lesson that the contemporary drive for a new mercantilism may be just as profoundly "reactionary," as profoundly opposed to the freedom and prosperity of the individual, as its pre-nineteenth-century ancestor.

---

1. "The laws and proclamations . . . were the product of conflicting interests of varying degrees of respectability. Each group, economic, social, or religious, pressed con-

stantly for legislation in conformity with its special interest. The fiscal needs of the crown were always an important and generally a determining influence on the course of trade legislation. Diplomatic considerations also played their part in influencing legislation, as did the desire of the crown to award special privileges, *con amore*, to its favorites, or to sell them, or to be bribed into giving them, to the highest bidders. . . . The mercantilist literature, on the other hand, consisted in the main of writings by or on behalf of 'merchants' or businessmen . . . tracts which were partly or wholly, frankly or disguisedly, special pleas for special economic interests. Freedom for themselves, restrictions for others, such was the essence of the usual program of legislation of the mercantilist tracts of merchant authorship." Jacob Viner, *Studies in the Theory of International Trade* (New York: Harper & Brothers, 1937), pp. 58–59.

2. Adam Smith, *An Inquiry into the Nature and Causes of the Wealth of Nations* (New York: Modern Library, 1937), p. 625.

3. See the laudatory "Note on Mercantilism" in Chapter 23 of John Maynard Keynes, *The General Theory of Employment, Interest, and Money* (New York: Harcourt, Brace, 1936).

4. Quoted in Viner, p. 38.

5. Quoted in Eli F. Heckscher, *Mercantilism* (2nd Edition, New York: Macmillan Co., 1955), II, pp. 208–209. Also see Edgar S. Furniss, *The Position of the Laborer in a System of Nationalism* (New York: Kelley and Millman, 1957), p. 41.

6. Quoted in Furniss, p. 41.

7. *Ibid.*

8. See Furniss, pp. 79–84.

9. *Ibid.*, p. 115.

10. Frank W. Fetter, "Economic Articles in the *Westminster Review* and their Authors, 1824–51," *Journal of Political Economy* (December 1962), p. 572.

11. See Frank W. Fetter, "The Economic Articles in the *Quarterly Review* and their Authors, 1809–52," *Journal of Political Economy* (February 1958), pp. 48–51.

12. Quoted in *Ibid.*, p. 62.

13. See Frank W. Fetter, "The Economic Articles in *Blackwood's Edinburgh Magazine*, and their Authors, 1817–1853," *Scottish Journal of Political Economy* (June 1960), pp. 91–96.

14. See the illuminating study by Dr. George A. Billias, *The Massachusetts Land Bankers of 1740* (University of Maine Bulletin, April 1959).

Adam Smith's Economics of Freedom

by John Montgomery

The reputation of Adam Smith's *The Wealth of Nations* has survived its bicentennial, which is not always the case with anniversaries of weighty scientific or literary works. But Smith's portrayal of the free-market economy remains the centerpiece of economic theory, often challenged but never replaced. And, even after the passage of more than two centuries, it clearly speaks to the economic dilemma of today.

To start with one misconception, economics did not begin with the great eighteenth-century Scotsman Adam Smith. Economic thought can be traced back through St. Thomas Aquinas all the way to Aristotle. Nor was Smith the first economist. In his time there was a group of theorists in France which anticipated some of his ideas. They are now known as the Physiocrats, except that they called themselves *economistes.* In England at the time many pamphlets, tracts, and books on economic questions were being written by businessmen, bankers, and scholars of various sorts. The dominant point of view then, mercantilism, thought of economics as strategy in the competition among trading nations. This first epoch of the "science" of economics did not begin with Adam Smith; it culminated in him.

What Smith did in the watershed year of 1776 was to come out with a great tome of a thousand pages with the abridged title of *The Wealth of Nations.* In time it was to become a blockbuster in economics and it has been called one of the world's truly great books. What Smith did in the book was to survey all the scattered ideas and writings about economics before him and then assemble them into a coherent whole which, for the first time, compelled the recognition that economics was and deserved to be a single, special field. In Adam Smith political economy, as it was known then, was the beginning of modern economic thought.

The complete title of his book was *An Inquiry into the Nature and Causes of the Wealth of Nations,* and that well describes his point of departure. Economic debate in the eighteenth century focused on the source of national wealth. Was it agriculture, labor, or commerce? The

---

John Montgomery, a newspaperman and writer on socioeconomic issues, wrote this for the January 1982 issue of *The Freeman*.

answer suggested by the quickening of business activity in England at the time was commerce.

Not Just Precious Metals, But All Items of Commerce

The mercantilists held that wealth was gold and silver, mostly acquired in foreign trade. But Smith saw it differently: Wealth was the nation's production of the "necessaries, comforts, and conveniences of life" or, as he also put it, the "annual produce of the land and the labor of the people." As for the source of this wealth, Smith started with what economists would call a "labor theory of value." For Smith and his followers, and for all Marxists to this day, human labor was the ultimate source of wealth.

Smith pointed out the great increase in human productivity yielded by what he called the "division of labor," that is, the growing practice of splitting up the job of making something into separate tasks assigned to different workers. In effect, he was describing an early stage in the development of mass production and, to illustrate it, he chose the pin factory of his time.

He asserted that "a workman not educated to this business . . . nor acquainted with the machinery employed in it . . . could scarce, perhaps, with his utmost industry, make one pin in a day, and certainly could not make twenty. But in the way in which this business is now carried on . . . one man draws out the wire, another straights it, a third cuts it, a fourth points it, a fifth grinds it at the top for receiving the head; to make the head requires two or three distinct operations; to put it on, is a peculiar business, to whiten the pins is another; it is even a trade by itself to put them into the paper; and the important business of making a pin is, in this manner, divided into about eighteen distinct operations, which, in some manufactories, are all performed by distinct hands, though in others the same man will sometimes perform two or three of them. I have seen a small manufactory of this kind where ten men only were employed, and where some of them consequently performed two or three distinct operations. But though they were very poor, and therefore but indifferently accommodated with the necessary machinery, they could, when they exerted themselves, make among them about twelve pounds of pins in a day. There are in a pound upwards of four thousand pins of a middling size. These ten persons, therefore, could make among them upwards of forty-eight thousand pins in a day."

Thus, Smith made his point about the productivity realized by means of the division of labor—and in a small shop employing ten men at the very beginning of the Industrial Revolution.

Smith went on to describe how the division of labor operated not just in a shop or factory but also in a whole national economy made up of diverse, specializing firms and industries in the different localities and regions, taking advantage of local differences in climate, soil, location, natural resources, the characteristics of the local population: all of those things which can make possible more efficient and lower-cost production of particular goods than can be accomplished elsewhere. And, similarly, Smith described an international division of labor in the production of commodities for foreign trade among the diverse nations and regions of the world.

Economic Growth

From that starting point, Smith went on to describe the system of production of goods in a national economy and outlined what he conceived of as the forces which led to the "progress of opulence," or what today would be called economic growth. He saw the production of material wealth, that is, of goods, as requiring three things: the division of labor, the widening and extension of markets for the goods produced, and increasing "stock," his term for production equipment, machinery and working capital.

In Smith's scheme, it was the accumulation of capital which led to the progress of opulence from an agricultural economy to manufacturing to commerce. The resulting increased output of food and other goods necessary to life permitted the survival of a larger population which, in turn, meant further extension of markets, a larger and more skilled labor force, and further accumulation of capital. In this way he saw the economy spiraling to higher and higher levels of development, raising the whole social order with it. It was an optimistic, almost buoyant view which was largely justified by the times he lived in but was not to survive its author by very long.

It was Adam Smith's description of how a market economy worked that was the starting point of a complex theoretical system that would become the new "science of economics." His theory of markets would be elaborated and refined by economists throughout the nineteenth century, and it has remained center stage in the twentieth century, at least in the negative sense of growing disagreement and retreat from it after the debacle of theory in the Great Depression. But the theory of markets is too central a part of economics to be quickly set aside, and much of modern economic debate has amounted to repeated attempts to dislodge it in favor of corrective or alternative formulations.

Market Pricing

In effect, Smith conceived of the economy of a nation as one vast whole with immense internal complexity but with interaction and interdependence of internal forces which were self-adjusting and self-regulating. In Smith's scheme the market was not a place but the totality of exchanges—that is, of buying and selling—of the products of all the different occupations and industries in the national economy. At the center of this were prices, constantly changing in accordance with the laws of supply and demand and, in turn, balancing supply and demand not just for goods but for the resources, both human and material, needed to produce them.

As for those resources—land, labor, and capital, needed in varying proportions to produce each good—their prices, mediated by supply and demand, directed them to those places and those employments where they would produce the most for the economy and the population as a whole. Of course, money spent by one person is money received by another. So, in Smith's system, those prices were also income: rent for the landlords, wages for laborers, and profits for the capitalists and businessmen. These people, making up the three great classes of the population of Great Britain in his time, divided up the total income generated by the national economy, which amounted to the prices paid for all of the goods and commodities produced—that is, for all the "necessaries, comforts, and conveniences" of the people, the sovereign consumers for whom the system operated.

The Role of the Businessman

In Smith's market theory people were not only the beneficiaries but the moving parts of the system: householders, workers, farmers, landowners, manufacturers, merchants, and traders, all of them rational economic men (and they were almost solely male at that time) who were free to pursue their own gain, the best return for their own contributions to the economic life of their communities and the country. To Smith, the capitalist businessmen, whom he referred to as "undertakers," were the key to the success of the system. For it was the "undertakers" who coordinated the movements and combinations of all the other participants in the economy for their best possible employments under existing conditions.

Smith mistrusted businessmen. In one of the best known passages in his book, he wrote: "People of the same trade seldom meet together, even for merriment and diversion, but the conversation ends in a conspiracy against the public, or in some contrivance to raise prices." But he gave them credit for being the savers who accumulated capital for new business ventures, without which there would be no economic growth. He wrote that in contrast to the workers, who were forced to spend all they earned on the necessaries, and the idle rich, who squandered their incomes on the comforts and conveniences, the capitalist businessmen put off immediate spending for consumption to some extent and set aside part of their profits for investment in future undertakings, with no guarantee that the capital they risked might not be lost in an unsuccessful venture.

Mobility and Competition

Smith set forth two linked and indispensable conditions to be met if the economic system he described were to work: There must be free movement for all in the system so that each man might seek the best opportunity for his labor or resources. And there must be free competition among all for the buyer's shilling, for markets, for labor, and for jobs. There must be no monopolies or combinations in restraint of trade or limiting entry into new fields, and no government-granted privileges for a favored few. Smith railed at the dense thicket of government regulations and restrictions of his time, which he saw as preventing the fluid and free movement of men and capital throughout the economy that was necessary for prosperity and growth.

Smith sensed an order in the economic universe, not imposed from above but somehow the outcome of the almost infinite number of transactions in the exchange economy. It has been said that the nature of this order was the "mystery" he set out to solve in his book. Instead of government direction of the economy as the source of that order, Smith came up with his famous metaphor of the "invisible hand." It was, he wrote, as though there were an invisible hand directing the efforts of everyone—even though each man was pursuing his own gain—in a way that promoted the interests of society as a whole.

It was not that Smith thought the invisible hand was tugging on puppet strings to guide the economic behavior of each individual. To him, the invisible hand was a metaphor for the workings of the market economy in the setting of the institutions of political and economic freedom. It was Providence, he thought, that had endowed mankind with the capacities and propensities which made possible such a society and such a system. Today, what Smith called the invisible hand might be thought of in cybernetic terms as "feedback loops"—for example, as market prices being regulated by negative feedback.

Smith knew, of course, that his ideal of the invisible hand operating in a completely free, purely competitive market economy was never a very realistic picture of an economy in the real world. But he contended that the more nearly the ideal was realized, the better the economy would work. And it was that ideal which was the unifying concept he applied to the wilderness of economic phenomena to reveal an underlying order.

A Self-Regulating Arrangement

By now the idea of the self-regulating economy is a familiar one, whether accepted or not. And many of the elements contained in the idea had been described before Smith put them all together. But how did he come up with the whole "vision" and what was its source? In effect, it was already at hand, in the climate of opinion and generally held ideas of that time—although in a different context.

In Smith's time the burgeoning commercial society of England was beginning to generate the Industrial Revolution, that great outburst of inventions which meant the end of the old system of hand-crafted production and ushered in the modern age of mass production in factories equipped with power-driven machinery. England was harnessing waterpower and steam. Soon to come were the giant textile mills in the north of England where uprooted country people, and their children, tended looms which disgorged immense quantities of cotton cloth for new world markets. In its "satanic mills," capitalism was to produce enormous quantities of goods and amass hitherto unattainable wealth—as well as great fortunes for a few.

It was this great national wealth which, in effect, bought and paid for the British Empire, financing the Royal Navy, the troops and the colonial administrations which would rule one-third of the world. But there was a vital question posed by capitalism, although the word was not yet then in currency. How was this incredible machine to be controlled? It was showing signs of becoming a juggernaut.

Smith had been professor of "moral philosophy" at Glasgow University in Scotland. Economics or, rather, political economy as it was known at the time, was still a branch of moral philosophy, which corresponded to the social sciences of today. Besides moral philosophy there was natural philosophy, the physical sciences.

The "Age of Enlightenment"

Eighteenth-century philosophers, in the "Age of Enlightenment," believed they were beginning to make sense of the world in the light of scientific thought, which had erupted in the century that preceded them. In the seventeenth century, Isaac Newton's theoretical physics with its concept of the physical universe as a mechanical system and its theory of the "natural laws" of the movements of the heavenly bodies had seemed to show a harmony in nature, a cosmos with all its parts reliably performing their appropriate functions in the overall smooth working of the whole.

Inspired by that concept, the men of the Enlightenment believed there were also natural laws governing man's behavior. The social and moral sciences of that time were finding in the world of man the possibility of a similar, harmonious human-social cosmos, a world of free individuals pursuing the satisfaction of their natural desires and in so doing acting in ways that would fit into an orderly system of natural social processes.

But, outside of the libraries and studies of the scholars of that time, there was change, ferment, and disorder all around. The iron constraints of medieval society had long since given way, and the Protestant Reformation had rejected the absolute authority over the individual of God's church. The people were beginning to ask questions about their lot; there was a growing clamor for personal liberties and a chance to get in on the new opportunities to make money. The social philosophers of the seventeenth century were forced to confront some less-than-theoretical questions: How does social order emerge from the potential chaos of an individualistic society? Is there a natural social order? What should be the role of government?

By Adam Smith's time these questions had brought an answer: a theory of liberal democracy which was believed to rest on natural law like the laws of the physical world. The theory harked back to the philosopher John Locke in the previous century and, along with many others, was advanced in Smith's time by his close friend and fellow Scottish philosopher David Hume.

According to the theory, each individual was a part of nature and therefore was endowed with "natural" rights: to life, liberty, and property. Further, he was endowed with God-given capacities and propensities which would flower in a society that served the best interests of all. To realize that society, a political system of the rule of law rather than of a few powerful men was required. The laws would provide even-handed justice, personal freedoms, minimal government, private property, the sanctity of private contracts, economic freedoms, and free trade, both domestic and foreign. In the kind of society made possible by such laws, free men would both compete with and cooperate with each other, exercising their rights to pursue their own visions and, at the same time, respecting the rights of others.

Classical Liberalism

This doctrine of classical liberalism was patterned after Newton's concept of the physical universe as a mechanical system embodying "natural laws"; the doctrine amounted to a similar vision, that of a human-social system also embodying natural laws. And, in much the same way, what Smith did in his theory of a liberal economy was to pattern it, too, after Newton's system, using quasi-gravitational mechanics to explain the workings of a self-regulating market economy. What made it possible for Smith to do this was his encyclopedic knowledge of economic history and his authoritative mastery of the economic life of his own time, which he described in realistic and convincing detail.

Classical liberalism provided the vision for political and social reforms in England for two centuries. By the twentieth century that time had largely passed in England and in the rest of Europe where intellectuals and social reformers were convinced by Marx's dissection of capitalism and excited by the utopian spell of socialism. But the Founding Fathers of this country were very much men of the Enlightenment and it was the ideas of classical liberalism as expressed in the Declaration of Independence and the Constitution that gave shape to the American republic and have been the foundation of our liberties ever since.

On publication, Adam Smith's great tome was well received by his fellow scholars both in Britain and abroad. But government, understandably, was in no hurry to take his advice, with one notable exception: The younger Pitt, to become George the Third's prime minister, was deeply influenced by the book as a student and would be the first English statesman to be converted to the doctrine of free trade.

Smith's death in 1790 attracted little notice. But the influence of his book continued to grow. By the time another twenty years had passed, his readers had become his followers and successors, and had established him as the father of classical economics. His book routed the mercantilist ideas that had prevailed in his lifetime and for a while virtually blotted out the memory of those who had come before him.

John Bright: Voice of Victorian Liberalism

by Nick Elliott

John Bright did more than anyone else to bring about the great advances for liberty in nineteenth-century Britain. A leading orator and agitator, he was considered by many to be the best political speaker of the century. His voice contained a quiet passion, that captivated fellow members of Parliament and roused the many thousands he addressed at public meetings.

Born in Rochdale (a town north of Manchester) in 1811, Bright was raised in the individualistic tradition of the Society of Friends. From the faith of his family, he learned that there is a natural equality of mankind, and that any individual can communicate with God. He later recognized this connection between his religion and his politics:

> We have no creed which monarchs and statesmen and high priests have written out for us. Our creed, so far as we comprehend it, comes pure and direct from the New Testament. We have no thirty-seven articles to declare that it is lawful for Christian men, at the command of the civil magistrate, to wear weapons and to serve in wars.[1]

For many years Nonconformists—those who did not conform to the established Church of England—had been persecuted and forced to finance the state church. Because of this, they also tended toward political individualism. John's father, Jacob Bright, was liberal in his politics, and a supporter of the radical Member of Parliament Joseph Hume. He was also one of the many Nonconformists who refused to pay the church rate—a local tax to finance the state religion—and as a result had silver spoons taken from his house by church officials.

As a young man, John worked in his father's cotton mill. He kept a collection of books in a room above the counting house, and in spare moments went there to expand his knowledge. His favorite writer was the poet and liberal scholar John Milton. At the same time, John was tutored in politics by his fellow workers, supporters of the Chartist

---

Mr. Elliott is a graduate of the University of York and currently a resident of London, England. This article was originally published in the August 1988 issue of *The Freeman*.

movement, which called for universal male suffrage and the elimination of property qualifications for members of Parliament.

Bright established his reputation in an 1840 debate over church rates, an issue close to his heart. In his hometown of Rochdale, he led a rebellion against the local vicar. A large gathering was held in the local churchyard, at which John mounted a tombstone to denounce the "foul connection" of church and state.

The Campaign Against the Corn Laws

Bright is most famous for his part in the successful campaign for the repeal of the corn laws. During the Napoleonic War, English landowners had enjoyed a monopoly in the production of food. At the end of the war, they instituted the corn laws—a form of import control—to protect their domestic monopoly from competition. The laws kept the price of grain high, and since bread was the primary sustenance for most families, the laws created particular hardship for the poor. The issue had been brewing for some time. Charles Villiers had proposed corn law repeal in Parliament every year, and the Anti-Corn Law League was formed in Manchester in 1839. Richard Cobden and John Bright were instrumental in its founding.

The campaign gathered impetus in the "hungry forties" with a succession of poor harvests. The poverty was very real—observers reported seeing people with "withered limbs" in Manchester. Cobden was elected to Parliament from Stockport, and Bright was elected in 1843 to represent Durham. The League developed into a highly efficient political machine with mass support. They distributed millions of leaflets, held gatherings up and down the country, and published their own newspaper, *The League*. In addition, they gained the support of the fledgling *Economist*. In 1845, when Ireland was struck by a potato blight, pressure for repeal grew even stronger.

Bright and Cobden embarked upon a hectic speaking tour. The climax was a meeting in the Covent Garden Theatre, where Bright railed against the protectors of upper class privilege: "The law is, in fact a law of the most ingeniously malignant character. . . . The most demoniacal ingenuity could not have invented a scheme more calculated to bring millions of the working classes of this country to a state of pauperism, suffering, discontent, and insubordination. . . ."[2]

Leading Whigs and Tories were convinced of the need for repeal, and on June 25, 1846, a bill for repeal was carried. The elimination of other import duties followed, and a 70-year era of British free trade began; in the popular mind, free trade now signified cheap bread.

The event was also a momentous one for the landscape of British politics. Division in the Tories was irreconcilable. The landowning interests had stubbornly resisted free trade, and Prime Minister Robert Peel, who had supported it, was forced to resign. The division excluded the conservatives from government for the next 20 years.

In his activity in support of free trade, Bright was motivated above all by a concern for the plight of ordinary people. From the same motive, he opposed all the legislation which regulated working conditions in factories. The Factory Act of 1847 was in part a retaliation by the landowners for the corn law repeal: regulation of factories was a means of penalizing manufacturers. Bright was certain that it would make people worse off by reducing the number of hours in which they could earn money.

Opposition to the Crimean War

In their campaign against the corn laws, Bright and Cobden rode a wave of public adoration. But in their opposition to the Crimean War, the contrast could not have been greater, for they had to endure derision from a jingoistic public. Despite this, they produced some of the most lucid statements of non-interventionist foreign policy ever made, and Bright contributed some of his most memorable oratory.

For Bright, Cobden, and other leaders of the "Manchester School," free trade was inseparable from a pacific foreign policy. Trade is based on mutual cooperation, and evokes goodwill among nations. They rejected the argument that foreign alliances were needed to enforce a "balance of power" in Europe, and warned that such alliances would drag Britain into future conflicts. The only people who would benefit from war were the "tax-eating" class—government bureaucrats. Common people would suffer from the burden of taxes to fund foreign adventures. Bright and Cobden reserved no cordiality for Liberal Party Prime Minister Palmerston, a notorious interventionist whose policies attracted the description of "gun-boat diplomacy."

As the war continued, Bright became deeply distressed by the loss of life: 22,000 British soldiers died, but only 4,000 in action; the rest died from malnutrition, exposure, and disease. His passionate speeches left a lasting impression on the House of Commons. His most famous words were these:

> The Angel of Death has been abroad throughout the land; you may almost hear the beating of his wings. There is no one, as when the first-born were slain of old, to sprinkle with blood the

lintel and the two sideposts of our doors, that he may spare and pass on; he takes his victims from the castle of the noble, the mansion of the wealthy, and the cottage of the poor and lowly.[3]

India and the American Civil War

At the end of the Crimean War, Bright suffered a nervous collapse, and was unseated in the general election. However, it was not long before he was returned as member for Birmingham, and with renewed energy he sought better government for India. Bright argued that the mutiny of 1857 was caused by the ineptitude of colonial government. Capable Indians were excluded from the administration of their own country, positions being allocated instead by personal favor. Bright assailed the economic management which imposed onerous taxes on the Indian peasantry, stunting development to maintain a vast, inefficient Indian civil service. He was ahead of his time in recognizing that Britain would not rule India forever. He also saw the potential for conflict in a country of "twenty nations, speaking twenty different languages," and argued for a confederacy of smaller states.

For many years, Bright had been an admirer of the United States—he was sometimes known in the House of Commons as the Honourable Member for the United States. He thought that the free and democratic style of government in America should be a model for Britain. When civil war erupted, Bright was concerned for the future of the republic, but allied himself with the cause of the North.

English liberals weren't unanimous in supporting the North. Cobden initially inclined toward the South, and *The Economist* sympathized with the South throughout. A humanitarian always, Bright supported the North because of the issue of slavery, which appalled him. In the early part of the war, when military intervention on the side of the South seemed likely, Bright urged neutrality. He also maintained a correspondence with the Chairman of the Senate Foreign Relations Committee, Charles Sumner. He encouraged caution and diplomacy; some of the letters he wrote to Sumner were read to President Lincoln.

It was always a matter of regret for Bright that he never visited North America. He maintained his admiration for the United States, and saw in it the potential of a great world power.

Parliamentary Reform

Before 1867, only 16 percent of British adult males had the right to vote. In the 1860s, Bright led a vigorous campaign for full manhood suffrage, secret ballots, and equal representation for industrial cities like Birmingham and Manchester.

He rested his case upon two principles. First, since working people must pay taxes and bear the impact of legislation, they should also have a voice in government. Second, he expressed faith in the decision-making ability of ordinary people. A frequent claim of reactionary conservatives was that common people are incapable of making important decisions. Bright reversed this and argued that progress had been achieved only by enforcing working class opinion. He was somewhat naive in supposing that a mass franchise would lead to low taxes, free trade, and a non-interventionist foreign policy.

With his ability to rouse passions, Bright's efforts in the campaign for electoral reform made him a formidable adversary of the Conservative government. Previous campaigns had often suffered from having the support of only one class, whereas Bright rallied the middle and working classes into unity. Ironically, in the same way as corn law repeal, reform was introduced by a Conservative prime minister. Benjamin Disraeli presided over the 1867 Reform Act, which enfranchised two million additional men and cleared the way for later reforms.

Later Years: Cabinet and Ireland

As a parliamentary back-bencher, Bright had been enormously influential. Nearing the end of his campaigning career, he entered William Gladstone's cabinet in 1868. He never was happy in assuming collective responsibility, and soon had cause to disagree with his government colleagues. The Forster Act of 1870 laid the foundations of state education, and it incorporated the teaching of state religion which was anathema to Bright. He wrote to Gladstone that it had done a "tremendous mischief" to the party.[4] After the 1880 election, Bright was again invited into government. Soon after, Britain initiated a war with Egypt, and Bright's objection was so great that he felt compelled to resign.

Ireland was another longstanding interest. Bright had been a personal friend of Irish reformer Daniel O'Connell, who had supported the Anti-Corn Law League. Bright took up the grievances of the Irish and, after O'Connell's death in 1847, was often their most persistent representative in Parliament. He rejected all attempts to impose the Church of England upon the native Catholics; instead he called for the withdrawal of this "symbol of conquest." The other issue was land policy: Irish agriculture had always been weak because large-scale English owners maintained idle lands, and because tenants scratched a precarious existence with no legal right of tenancy. Bright offered three solutions: an end to the law of primogeniture which ensured the continuation of concentrated ownership; compensation for evicted tenants and loans for those who wanted to buy land; and land purchase from English owners, to be sold at a discount to Irish buyers.

Some of these proposals were implemented, as Gladstone had been taking note of Bright's suggestions. But in Parliament the Irish National representatives became increasingly militant. They used disruptive techniques which led, in response, to the rules of procedure which still are with us today. Bright deplored all this, and it significantly changed his attitude. In 1886, Gladstone introduced a land-purchase scheme to buy out the English landlords, along with a proposal for Irish home rule. By this time, Bright was so disgusted with the activities of the Nationalists in Parliament that he opposed the land-purchase scheme, and he regarded home rule as a policy which would endanger the "Protestant and loyal people of the north."[5]

As a figure of importance among the Liberals, Bright's opposition was very damaging to Gladstone. Home rule was defeated, and the Liberals were hopelessly divided on the issue. It pained Bright to speak out against Gladstone because they had been good friends.

In an essay of this length, it isn't possible to describe all of Bright's arguments. He opposed capital punishment, spoke on many aspects of colonial government, and addressed a variety of issues involving religious freedom. His speeches are a pleasure to read; one can imagine the impact they made upon listeners.

Bright lived from 1811 to 1889, and when looking at the political events during those years, the advance of liberal principles is quite momentous. In 1819, when demonstrators protested against the corn laws and the lack of parliamentary representation, they were cut down by a cavalry charge. As late as 1859, Queen Victoria expressed her concern to Lord Palmerston that John Bright was attempting to undermine British institutions. Yet by 1868, when Bright became the first Nonconformist to hold a cabinet post, he was respected, as were the principles he enunciated. In the campaign against the corn laws, he helped to establish free trade as a popular principle, which no politician would dare to interfere with for years to come. His stand with Cobden against the Crimean War inspired a later generation of liberals to follow the idea of non-intervention. Opening up Parliament to the scrutiny of ordinary people marked an end to the high-handed government of earlier times. In these, as in many other issues, John Bright, as a consistent and principled defender of individual liberty, imparted a widespread and lasting acceptance of liberal politics.

1. William Robertson, *The Life & Times of John Bright* (London: Fisher Unwin, 1912), p. 203.

2. Speech at Covent Garden Theatre, December 19, 1845, in J.E. Thorold Rogers, ed., *Speeches on Questions of Public Policy* (London: Macmillan, 1878), pp. 419–420.

3. Speech to the House of Commons, February 23, 1855, in Rogers, p. 251.

4. Quoted in G.M. Trevelyan, *The Life of John Bright* (London: Constable, 1913), p. 409.

5. Quoted in Keith Robbins, *John Bright* (London: Routledge & Kegan Paul, 1979), p. 256.

Richard Cobden:
Creator of the Free Market

by John Chodes

The first half of the nineteenth century in England was much like contemporary America: It was a country strangled by bureaucratic regulations. Many people were always hungry, not because of poverty-level wages, but because the price of grain for bread was kept artificially high by laws which simultaneously prevented the importation of foreign grain and subsidized domestic producers. Food riots, domestic unrest, and a stagnating economy were not sufficiently frightening to make the government eliminate these barriers.

In the midst of all this lived a successful young Manchester textile manufacturer named Richard Cobden. He saw the social injustice, and it made him furious. He was determined to change it, and he did. As a result, the world owes the existence of the free market to him. Cobden demonstrated methods that we can use to break down our own protectionist "fair trade" laws and massive food subsidies.

Richard Cobden began his public life by leaving his calico printing company to his brother. He received a portion of the profits, which allowed Cobden to devote full time to the cause of free trade. It seemed an impossible task. Yet, seven years later, England had undergone a revolutionary economic, political, and social change. Taxes on grain had been decimated. Unequaled prosperity flooded England. For the next 85 years Britain maintained world economic leadership, and the rallying cry of "free trade" became much more than an economic slogan. Free trade denoted the philosophy of limited government, social justice, and freedom.

Cobden understood the moral truths behind unregulated commerce. Breaking down barriers to trading freedom broke down class barriers and obstacles to civil rights. It reduced military expansion, since a powerful navy was a legacy from the old mercantile idea that warships protected trade between colonies and other controlled markets.

John Chodes is the Communications Director of the Libertarian Party of New York City. This article was originally published in the March 1993 issue of *The Freeman*.

The Corn Laws

Protectionist tariffs were called "Corn Laws." They restricted the free flow of corn, wheat, barley, and oats between Great Britain and foreign countries to shield the British farmer from competition.

Systematic government interference in grain production began in the 1660s. The amended Corn Law of 1774, which controlled legislation for the next half century, is a typical example: when the domestic price of corn, as paid to the farmer by the baker or dealer, fell below £2.4 a quarter (28 pounds), the farmer was encouraged to sell his products abroad, to prevent the market price from falling still further. He was given a bounty of five shillings for each "quarter" exported. When corn sold for £2.8, export was forbidden. At prices between these levels, there was a duty of six pence a quarter. Over time, this system became progressively more bureaucratized, with elaborate regulations specifying how and in what town the price was to be measured, with specific procedures for reporting and allowances for regional differences.[1]

The Corn Laws displayed another characteristic of government controls: Regulations and subsidies in one area led to manipulation in other areas. In this case, when bad harvests triggered soaring grain and bread prices, the Corn Law mechanism exacerbated the problem, causing still higher prices. This provoked civil disturbances to the point where the government feared insurrection. To defuse the threat, workers' wages were subsidized, relative to the price of bread. This subsidy came from the "Poor Rates," the nineteenth-century British welfare system. This greatly expanded state entitlement programs, leading to massive fraud, inequities, and even greater civil unrest.

The Corn Laws are not merely things of the past. Their spirit exists in most countries of the world. In the U.S. today, agricultural products are subsidized and stored, to the tune of tens of billions of dollars annually, to keep the price of food artificially high. This enhances the farmer's income but it also prevents the poor from eating as they should. This has led, as in nineteenth-century England, to protectionism, international tensions, and the threat of trade wars.

Richard Cobden: Businessman to Pamphleteer

Cobden was born in Dunford, West Sussex, in 1804. Because of a succession of family business failures, his father could not support young Richard. He went to live with an uncle who trained him to be a clerk in his London warehouse. At 21 Cobden became a traveling salesman. He was so successful that in 1831 he went out on his own and took over the calico printing company in Manchester.

Manchester was the world's first great industrial city. It was viewed as the metropolis of the future. Alexis de Tocqueville best explained the paradox of Manchester: "From this foul drain the greatest stream of human industry flows out to fertilize the whole world. From this filthy sewer pure gold flows. Here humanity attains its most complete development and its most brutish; here civilization works its miracles, and civilized man is turned back almost into savage."[2]

In Manchester, Cobden had his first lesson as to what free trade meant. As he assumed ownership of the company, the protective tariff on calicos was repealed, making it possible to export them competitively. This opened up vast new markets that could not exist before, allowing Cobden to develop a new kind of international selling strategy. Cobden "introduced a new mode of business. The custom of the calico trade at that period was to print a few designs, and watch cautiously and carefully those which were most acceptable to the public, when larger quantities of those which seemed to be preferred would be printed off and offered to the retail dealer. . . . Cobden and his partners did not follow the cautious and slow policy of their predecessors, but fixing themselves upon the best designs, they had those printed off at once and pushed the sale energetically throughout the country. Those pieces which failed to take in the home market were at once shipped to other countries and the consequence was that the associated firms became very prosperous."[3]

Yet, at the height of his achievements, Cobden's interest in calico waned. He was eager to pursue other courses. By 1835 he wrote his first political pamphlets. One, called "Russia" (describing the threat of Russia against the decaying Turkish Empire), contained the core of this mature thought: "It is labor improvements and discoveries that confer the greatest strength upon a people. By these alone and not by the sword of the conqueror, can nations in modern and all future times hope to rise to power and grandeur."[4]

Cobden wrote that England's rulers inhibited discovery and improvements by wasting millions on the military. His favorite target was Britain's obsession with the doctrine of the balance of power. He saw it as a source of conflict, not stability. "Empires have arisen unbidden by us; others have departed despite our utmost efforts to preserve them."[5]

Cobden's ideas were not idealistic dreams. The United States' industrial strength had revolutionized the world economy and political equilibrium. Cobden: "The new world is destined to become the arbiter of the commercial policy of the old."[6] Already the need to trade with America had compelled Britain to abandon many regulations governing colonial commerce.

Since free trade and military non-intervention were the same to Cobden, he pleaded for Britain to abandon the past and repeal protectionism. This would make Britain "turn moralist, in the end, in self-defense."[7]

Manchester Incorporation: Prelude to Repeal

Cobden's pamphlets attracted the attention of the editor of the *Manchester Times*, Archibald Prentice, who asked him to speak on free trade. This led to Cobden's being elected to the Manchester Chamber of Commerce. Here he met two men who would influence his thinking and direction: John Benjamin "Corn Law" Smith and John Bright. Smith's nickname was due to his years of singlehandedly fighting for Corn Law repeal, long before it became a major topic. It was Smith who converted Cobden to total repeal, not just incremental reductions. John Bright became Cobden's chief lieutenant in the long war for repeal. Bright's speaking tours around the country helped lead to victory.

Cobden used the Chamber of Commerce as a vehicle for focusing public issues. The first political problem he tackled was the incorporation of Manchester. Like many of England's new industrial cities, Manchester had no borough (an urban political administrative area) charter. Its government was manorial, with the power of a small town, instead of one of England's largest urban centers.

In 1837 Cobden led the battle for a charter. One factor in winning was that he fought for it as if it were a national issue. His pamphlet, "Incorporate Your Borough," portrayed the struggle as one of democracy versus privilege, the rights of the productive classes against the rapacious aristocracy. He showed that the nobility's gerrymandering of counties forced the middle and working classes to be their vassals.

Incorporation required a petition of taxpayers. There was powerful opposition from the upper class Tories. To counter this, Cobden focused on the "shopocracy," the smaller merchants and manufacturers, for petition signatures. Then, using electoral registers, the Incorporationists sent a circular to all parliamentary electors who supported reform causes, to aid them by filling seats at public meetings. They did, and incorporation passed despite the fact that the Tories had three times as many signatures. Cobden made a name-by-name check of the opposition petition and found that 70 percent were invalid. With incorporation, Cobden was elected to his first public offices: borough councilor and alderman.[8]

The Manchester League: Fighting for Free Trade

Cobden now set his sights on an ambitious national goal that had previously proved impossible to attain: repeal of the Corn Laws. In 1838 the Manchester Anti-Corn Law Association (later, the Manchester League) was created. Cobden saw repeal as the greatest single battle of his time. It would unite workers, farmers, and commercial interests against privilege to radically alter the political-power structure of the country.

The League's initial goal was to educate the public. Lecturers went all around England, giving free-trade conferences. At this stage, political pressure did not seem necessary. But the League did have an ally in Parliament: Charles Villiers. For years he had unsuccessfully tried to initiate a Corn Law repeal debate in the House of Commons, which was dominated by big landlords. However, Cobden knew that Villiers' efforts helped identify supporters at the national level. This would influence the League's strategy in the provinces.

Within the first year Cobden realized that he had underestimated the Protectionists' strength. In rural areas, League meetings were disrupted by physical violence. The farmers erroneously believed that free trade would bring unemployment and depression. The Chartists, representing the urban workers, were hostile for the same reason. Cobden hoped that the League's message would convince both groups that repeal would open up new markets, which would raise all wages. It required years of educating for these truths finally to be perceived.

This generated a strategic change: the lectures were now combined with petition drives for Parliament. Thus began overt political activism. By 1840 the Manchester League transformed itself, creating in every borough an anti-Corn Law party, or at least an effort to "prevent the return of any candidate at the next election, whatever his political party may be, who supports . . . the landowner's bread tax."[9] This meant a more aggressive League, less compromising, less fearful of making enemies.

In 1841, a major economic depression occurred. Suddenly Prime Minister Robert Peel resorted to the free-trade idea of lower tariffs to stimulate the economy. This made the Corn Laws nationally significant and gave greater credibility to the League.

By now the League had several members in Parliament, including

Cobden. But he was a reluctant member. He did not want to be a "party man," loyal and compromising. He needed to be free to harass the government.

Cobden's speeches in Parliament were not influential and this dampened League members' enthusiasm. Support dropped sharply. In all mass movements, zeal is critical. There is a constant need to exceed earlier achievements or risk dissolution. So Cobden created "make-work" projects like conferences and fund-raisers to keep the fervor at high pitch.

By 1843, paradoxically, economic recovery made the League acceptable to the one group most antagonistic to repeal: the aristocratic landowners. When times had been bad, high prices and high subsidies compensated for the poor yields. But now, prices kept falling with increased abundance, and the Tories saw that the Corn Laws did not shore up their incomes.

Cobden's speeches became more moderate. Instead of attacking the Corn Laws, he attacked the greater evils behind them: the economic woes to workingmen and farmers. The new accent was on distress, not repeal. Now he no longer seemed menacing to the Tories. Gone were the threats of the collapse of society because of high food prices. No longer did he say that the Corn Laws benefited only the rich. He appealed to the landlords themselves, showing them that protective tariffs deterred them from investing to improve their crops, thus hindering their prosperity.

This wider view drew many leading Tories to the repeal side and was responsible for Robert Peel receiving a League delegation after repeatedly turning them down.

This was followed by a new League political plan. All the boroughs were classified as either "safe," "doubtful," or "hopeless." Voter registration focused on the hopeless districts. Teams of lecturers and voter canvassers fanned out and recruited thousands of new members. Cobden's overall objective was staggering: to reach every voter with League material through the canvassers. The sheer scale of it produced more enthusiasm, more fund raisers, more activities, but it failed and did not destroy the Protectionists. Cobden had the courage to admit he was wrong and turned around completely in mid-campaign, refocusing on the winnable boroughs.

Cobden targeted 160 boroughs as winnable. The 1845 national election showed substantial gains in 112. This still wasn't sufficient to win a Parliamentary vote. League members were now thoroughly demoralized. Their tremendous work seemed futile. Then Cobden discovered a loophole in the election law, enabling the League to attack from an entirely different direction. This proved to be the key to victory.

Previously Cobden had conceded the counties (the rural political districts). To win them he would have to create a vast new electorate. This seemed impossible because of the large property qualification required. Or so he thought. But a little-known law made it possible to vote in a county election if one owned a "forty-shilling freehold," a small piece of property that almost anyone could afford. By promoting forty-shilling freeholds as a great real estate investment, the number of free-trade voters was greatly expanded. Immediately the Tories retreated. They acknowledged that protectionism hindered agricultural modernization and conceded that subsidies did not stabilize corn prices.

Seeing that his opponents were caving in, Cobden once again switched the mode of attack: de-emphasizing public education to put more pressure on Parliament. This forced Prime Minister Peel over to the League side, provoking a governmental crisis. He was forced to resign and his government collapsed. Repeal now seemed within reach. But the chaos compelled a Parliamentary reorganization, reflecting the revolutionary change in the balance of power that repeal represented, shifting away from the aristocrats toward the urban middle class. It appeared that the Protectionists had formed a last-ditch coalition to block repeal just when it seemed assured. League members held their breath. Repeal passed Parliament and became law.[10]

The Consequences of Repeal

Following repeal, Richard Cobden was physically, mentally, and financially drained. He considered retiring permanently from politics. For the five years prior to repeal he saw very little of his wife and children. "My only boy is five years old. . . . [H]e did not positively know me as his father, so incessantly was I upon the tramp."[11] Yet Cobden felt the necessity to go on. He saw repeal as a beginning, not an end. More than prosperity, it would bring world peace. He spent the next fourteen months on a missionary tour of Europe, promoting the social benefits of trade without barriers.

He wrote: "Warriors and despots are generally bad economists and they instinctively carry their ideas of force and violence into the civil politics of their governments. Free trade is a principle which recognizes the paramount importance of individual action."[12]

Several years later his evangelism led to the second great triumph of his political career, the Anglo-French Commercial Treaty of 1860. France was still a protectionist country, but Cobden's tour had converted important Frenchmen into free traders. They had even influenced Napoleon III. One such person was Michel Chevalier, a political economist.

For centuries England and France had been military antagonists, but in the Crimean War of 1854–55 they were allies. Through free trade there was a unique opportunity to strengthen the bonds for permanent peace.

Initially there were several secret meetings in London among Chevalier, Cobden, and Gladstone, the Chancellor of the Exchequer. Then Cobden, with no official status, quietly left for Paris. He believed then, as always, that free trade would undo the national animosities kept alive by the professional diplomats and the military. "I would not step across the street just now to increase our trade, for the mere sake of commercial gain. . . . But to improve moral and political relations of France and England, by bringing them into greater intercourse and increased dependence, I would walk barefoot from Calais to Paris."[13]

Napoleon realized that he had to convince his own government about the benefits of free trade. He asked Cobden how to go about it. Cobden replied, "I told him, I would act precisely as I did in England, by dealing first with one article which was the keystone of the whole system. In England, that article was corn, in France, it was iron; that I should totally abolish and at once the duty on pig iron, and leave only a small revenue duty, if any, on bars . . . this would render it much easier to deal with all the other industries, whose general complaint is that they can't compete with England owing to the high price of iron and coal."[14]

When the negotiations reached their critical phase, Cobden thought he would be replaced by professional diplomats. Instead he was given plenipotentiary powers and continued on his own. The agreement was signed in January 1860.

Cobden's Legacy

Cobden died in April 1865. He was 60 years old. His legacy is enormous and remains so to this day. For 85 years free trade reigned as England's national policy, influencing the commercial principles of every major country in the world. Richard Cobden's idealism and passionate dream can be summed up by his statement: "I see in the free trade principle that which will act on the moral world as the principle of gravitation in the universe—drawing men together, thrusting aside the antagonisms of race, and creeds and language, and uniting us in the bonds of eternal peace. . . . I believe the effect will be to change the face of the world, so as to introduce a system of government entirely distinct from that which now prevails. I believe the desire and the motive for large and mighty empires and gigantic armies and great navies . . . will die away . . . when man becomes one family, and freely exchanges the fruits of his labor with his brother man."[15]

1. Norman Longmate, *The Breadstealers* (New York: St. Martin's Press, 1984), pp. 3–4.

2. Alexis de Tocqueville, *Journeys to England and Ireland,* edited by J.P. Mayer (New Haven, Conn: Yale University Press, 1958), pp. 107–108.

3. John McGilchrist, *Richard Cobden, the Apostle of Free Trade* (New York: Harper & Brothers, 1865), p. 20.

4. Richard Cobden, "Russia," from *The Political Writings of Richard Cobden,* 4th edition (London: W. Ridgway, 1903), p. 26.

5. Cobden, "America," from *Political Writings,* p. 5.

6. Cobden, p. 21.

7. Cobden, p. 256.

8. Nicholas Edsall, *Richard Cobden, Independent Radical* (Cambridge: Harvard University Press, 1986), pp. 51–59.

9. Cobden, p. 85.

10. Edsall, pp. 53–153.

11. Edsall, p. 174.

12. Edsall, p. 186.

13. Edsall, p. 333.

14. Edsall, p. 334.

15. Richard Cobden, *Speeches on Public Policy, By Richard Cobden, M.P.,* edited by John Bright and J.E. Thorold Rogers (London: Macmillan & Co., 1870), pp. 225–226.

The Legacy of Karl Marx

by Henry Hazlitt

A number of women (and men) have recently been contending that women who are just as productive as men are being employed on the average for only about 70 percent as much pay, and that the statistics prove it.

I am not going to quarrel with the comparisons of men's and women's actual wages, but with the contention about productivity. In a market in which competition is permitted between employers and between workers, the situation ascribed could not long exist. What would prevent it, what does prevent it, is the selfishness of employers.

Let us suppose that there was an industry in which both male and female workers were producing enough to bring the employer an ascertainable added profit of just over $10 an hour, but in which the men workers were receiving $10 an hour, and the equally productive women workers only $7 an hour.

It would soon occur to an unscrupulously selfish employer that he should henceforth employ only women workers from which he could make a net $3 more an hour than from his male workers. He would let his men workers go. Other employers would follow his example, and for the same reason. But this would mean that the female workers would start demanding higher individual wages until their pay was on an equality with that previously received by males.

In other words, selfish employers would prefer to make only $2 an hour net by employing female labor at $8 an hour rather than see competing employers make $3 net out of them. They would even choose to make only $1 an hour net by paying them $9 an hour rather than stand by and watch other employers making $2 net out of them. This would continue until prevailing female wages in that industry were very close to female labor productivity in dollar terms. (In the long run, of course,

Henry Hazlitt (1894–1993), noted economist, author, editor, reviewer, and columnist, was well known to readers of the *New York Times*, *Newsweek*, *The Freeman*, *Barron's*, *Human Events*, and many other publications. Best known of his books are *Economics in One Lesson*, *The Failure of the "New Economics*," *The Foundations of Morality*, and *What You Should Know About Inflation*. This article was originally published in the March 1986 issue of *The Freeman*.

there would be no drop in the prevailing men's pay, because their productivity would still make it profitable to employ them at that rate.)

To state this more briefly and bluntly, any employer would be a fool to hire male workers for $10 an hour when he could hire equally productive women workers for $7 an hour.

There are, it is true, special conditions, temporary and localized, in which labor productivity might not be the dominant factor in determining wage levels. In a small mill town, for example, in which there was only one mill, not large enough to employ the entire working population, the wages paid by that mill might fall below the worker-productivity level. But this would tend to prove only a temporary situation. Two developments would be likely to change it. The unemployed surplus workers would start to leave for other towns. And the mill owners would be tempted to reinvest their profits and expand their operations.

So far, I have been writing about the factors that tend to eliminate wage discrimination on sexual grounds where it exists. But the same considerations would also tend to eliminate wage discrimination on grounds of color, race, nationality, or other reasons. Where such wage differences persist, they tend to reflect real differences in productivity.

Let me now carry my contention a giant step further. The selfishness of individual employers is the force that, under competitive capitalism, brings the level of wages up close to the full value of the productivity of the workers.

Of course, there are never conditions of perfect competition; of full knowledge on both sides, employer and employed, of their respective opportunities. There are individual accidents, immobilities, prejudices, and other factors that prevent everybody's wage or salary from corresponding with the approximate value of his or her contribution or output. But this correspondence is the dominant long-run *tendency.*

There is nothing original in this explanation. I have simply been stating, in fact, in an unusual form, what is known as the marginal productivity theory of wages. This is the theory held by the overwhelming majority of serious economists today.

The Marginal Productivity Theory of Value

This theory was astonishingly late in its development. It did not make its appearance until the very end of the nineteenth century, in the principal works of the Austrian economists Carl Menger (1871), Friedrich von Wieser (1884), and Eugen von Böhm-Bawerk (1884), and of the American economist John Bates Clark (1899).

Why did its development take so long? It took so long partly because the field was already occupied by other theories—wrong theories. And how did they in turn get started? They got started partly through the errors of writers that were in some respects acute and even profound thinkers. The first of these was the economist David Ricardo (1772–1823), who, by abstract reasoning, developed a labor theory of value in which the contributions of capital investment, initiative, invention, and management somehow got buried.

Then, along came Karl Marx. Ostensibly taking off from Ricardo, he presented a pure "exploitation" theory of wages, and declared outright that as long as the "capitalist system" continued in existence there could be no real improvement in the condition of workers.

This assertion was made in the face of some very noticeable improvement in the economic condition of the "masses" before 1848, when the *Communist Manifesto* was published, and certainly in the remaining 35 years of Marx's life.

Doubtless there was some excuse for Marx's failure to notice this improvement. In the early years of his life some relics of the medieval system were still around. Great tracts of land were still held by princes, dukes, and barons, and the men who tilled the soil were often forced to pay excessive rents. Production was by our present standards incredibly low. Capital goods—tools, implements, machinery, vehicles, and other equipment—were still rare, crude and primitive. There was a scarcity of donkeys, horses, and other farm animals. On the farms, human beings were forced to carry great burdens on their own backs, as they still do in China today. Only very slowly were more capital goods produced. The great bulk of labor went into producing tomorrow's food and other necessities.

But let us now turn to the actual text of the *Communist Manifesto*. That document, of approximately 40 pages, was written by Karl Marx and Friedrich Engels partly as a call for civil war—"Working men of all countries, unite!"—partly as propaganda, and partly to explain the economic theories of Communism to the workers. But the reader will look in vain to find those theories spelled out in any reasoned form.

We are told that there are two main classes in society—the "proletariat," which consists of the "workers," employed and unemployed, and forms allegedly about nine-tenths of the population, and the "bourgeoisie," which consists of the employers and a few other groups who are comfortably well off. The bourgeoisie rule. They hire the proletariat; and because they do, they necessarily "exploit" them. The only way this dreadful situation can be changed is by revolution, in which the proletariat must seize all the property of the bourgeoisie, and, if they object, kill them.

The Marxist Exploitation Dogma

No explanation is offered in the *Manifesto* of how this "exploitation" is possible, or what is its exact extent. The word implies that the employers pay their workers only a fraction of what they are worth—of what they add to production or profits. The fraction is not mentioned. Let us say it is only 50 percent. As individual employers would be making such a big profit at that rate, and would obviously want to hire workers away from other employers, what stops them? The exploitation theory implies that the employers must all be in some secret agreement to keep wages down to this existing near-starvation level, and maintain it through the most drastic penalties against humane employers, if any, who attempt to offer more. "The average price of wage-labor is the minimum wage, i.e., that quantum of the means of subsistence which is absolutely requisite to keep the laborer in bare existence as a laborer."

All this is pure fiction. The exploitation theory implies that the wage-level cannot rise. In trying to maintain this, the *Manifesto* quickly falls into inconsistencies and self-contradictions. We are told that: "The bourgeoisie, by the rapid improvement of all instruments of production . . . draws even the most barbarian nations into civilization. The cheap prices of its commodities are the heavy artillery with which it batters down all Chinese walls. . . . The bourgeoisie, during its rule of scarce one-hundred years, has created more massive and more colossal productive forces than have all preceding generations together," with "whole populations conjured out of the ground."

But this enormously increased production could not have been possible without equally increased consumption. The increased population that the increased production made possible must have consisted mainly of the proletarians, and the increased production itself could only have taken place in response to an increased demand. This demand must have been made possible by increased purchasing power, and that in turn either by increased wages or lower prices. But nowhere in the *Manifesto* is this necessary chain of causation acknowledged. The exploitation dogma blinded Marx to the obvious.

The *Manifesto* keeps compounding its economic errors. Obviously capital—which is most usefully thought of as capital goods—is used because it increases production. And because it increases production, it must increase the income of the owner or user. The carpenter would get nowhere without the use of hammers, saws, chisels, and even more elaborate machinery. And so for all other artisans. These tools and machines must at least promise to "pay for themselves" before they are acquired.

Yet we find the authors of the *Manifesto* writing: "In proportion as *the use of machinery* and division of labor *increases,* in the same proportion the burden of toil *increases,* whether by prolongation of the working hours, by increase in the work exacted in a given time, or by increased speed of the machinery, etc." [My italics.] Even if the reduction in weekly working hours recorded through the years did not show this *Manifesto* statement to be false, it was nonsense on its face. Yet Marx and Engels go on: "Machinery obliterates all distinctions of labor, and *reduces* wages to the same level!" [My italics.]

The Historical Record

From the 1830s on, however, the historic record shows a reduction of hours and an increase of wages from the introduction of machinery. Professor W. H. Hutt, in "The Factory System of the Early Nineteenth Century," writes: "That the apparent benefits wrought by the early Factory Acts are largely illusory is suggested by the steady improvement which was undoubtedly taking place before 1833, partly as a result of the development of the factory system itself." (*Capitalism and the Historians,* edited by F.A. Hayek [Chicago: University of Chicago Press, 1954], p. 181.)

Tooke and Newmarch, in their book *A History of Prices From 1792 to 1856,* publish extracts from a report issued by the City Chamberlain of Glasgow in 1856. This records that in 1856 wages of skilled labor in the building trades (masons, carpenters, and joiners) increased 20 percent from the level of 1850–51, and wages of unskilled labor 48 percent in the same period. He attributes this principally to "increased production in consequence of improvements in machinery."

"It must also be borne in mind," he adds, "that weavers and spinners worked 69 hours per week in 1841 and only 60 hours in 1851–56, and hence received in 1851–56 more money for less labor." He also notes at another point that in 1850: "The number of hours per week worked by masons, carpenters and other artisans employed in the building trades was 60 hours, or six days of 10 hours each, with a deduction of 1½ hours for meals. Since 1853, the weekly time has been reduced to 57 hours."

For the United States (which seems to have lagged greatly behind England), the official publication, *Historical Statistics of the U.S.: Colonial*

Times to 1957, reports (p. 90) that in 1860, the weighted average of working hours in all industries was 11 hours a day (Monday through Saturday inclusive), and that by 1891 this had fallen to 10 hours. In 1890, the working week was 60 hours (6 times 10 daily) and by 1926 had fallen to 50.3.

Recent issues of government publications, the annual *Statistical Abstract* and the current monthly *Economic Indicators*, show that the average of manufacturing hours fell from 51 a week in 1909 to 39.8 in 1957 and to 35 in 1985. Thus average working hours per week under capitalism, in other words, show a steady fall for nearly a century and a half.

In the *Manifesto*, our two authors mention frequently how "the competition between the workers" undermines solidarity and reduces wages. But they never once acknowledge the existence of competition among employers for workers. It is precisely this that brings wages up to the value of the workers' specific contribution to output. And this is not because the employers have or need to have any altruistic motives, but simply the motive of maximizing their own individual profits.

The Ominous Appeal of Hatred

Karl Marx must himself later have felt a great deal of misgiving about the lack of any real explanation of the maleficent workings of the existing economic system that he had portrayed in the *Manifesto*. For in 1867 he published (in Germany) a volume entitled *Das Kapital*. This was apparently intended to be the first of further volumes, but though Marx lived to 1883, nothing more appeared. Some commentators have surmised that Marx had reached an impasse, and could not decide how to continue. After Marx died, Engels undertook to "complete" the work in three volumes by supplementing his friend's unfinished manuscripts. The Austrian economist Eugen von Böhm-Bawerk thoroughly demolished the argument of the finished work in his *Karl Marx and the Close of His System* (1896), a masterful refutation that does not have to be done again.

Let me remind the reader once more that the thesis with which I began this piece—that the assumption of pure selfish competition on the part of the employers would be enough to explain how workers on the average receive practically the full value of their productive contribution—is only a novel way of presenting the marginal productivity theory of wages, now accepted by the overwhelming majority of present-day economists.

The factual substantiation of that theory is particularly impressive in the United States. The annual report of nonfinancial corporation earnings, going back for more than 30 years, show that the employees today receive an average of about 90 percent of corporate gross earnings in their wages and the stockholders only about 10 percent in their profits. In fact, a man's personal income often seems to have little to do with whether he is technically an employee or an employer. A baseball, football, basketball, or prize-fighting star may receive an income in the million-dollar range, far above that of the promoter who technically employs him. It is a result of the star's "productivity"—his box-office appeal. It is the competition among promoters, employers, that brings this about.

Selfish Capitalists vs. the Communist Manifesto

From the standpoint of common sense, the appeal of the *Manifesto* to violence and class war seems entirely needless. If the proletariat (supposedly some nine-tenths of the population) would be better off under a Communist economy, all that was necessary was to make this clear to them, and they could be trusted to vote themselves into power and such an economy into being. (Democracy was emerging in Britain in 1848, and, for whites, already functioning in America.)

But such an appeal gave little promise of starting a "movement" or leading to early political action. Marx and Engels were agitators, activists—and shrewd psychologists. They knew that most people who find themselves at the bottom of the economic ladder are tempted to put the blame, not on themselves, but mainly on somebody else. The exploitation theory, however weak as an economic doctrine, was tremendously persuasive psychologically and as a call for action. It was an essential part of their propaganda.

So, though the *Communist Manifesto*, even in its own time, failed completely as an economic guidebook, it did succeed thoroughly in instilling class hatred. This hatred, unfortunately, has been its most permanent contribution. It was originally directed ostensibly against a special class, the bourgeoisie—the employers, and all those comparatively well off—in revenge for "exploiting" the workers.

But, with the passing years, the target of this hatred has been quietly changed. As the employing class in Russia was liquidated by various means, a still existing group had to be substituted. To stay in command, a dictatorship must continue to point to a powerful enemy to be feared and destroyed. Fortunately, such an enemy can still be pointed to. It is the "capitalist" nations as a whole, especially the United States. Decades after the Bolshevik Revolution, most of the American population is notably better off than the population in the Soviet Union. Though Russian school children were long taught that we were an "imperialist" nation, the American "proletariat" came to be tacitly included, as the Russian "bourgeoisie" once explicitly were, among the people to be envied and somehow blamed for the plight of the Communist-ruled countries.

II. THE INDUSTRIAL REVOLUTION
AND ITS CONSEQUENCES

Facts About the
"Industrial Revolution"

by Ludwig von Mises

It is generally asserted that the history of modern industrialism and especially the history of the British "Industrial Revolution" provide an empirical verification of the "realistic" or "institutional" doctrine and utterly explode the "abstract" dogmatism of the economists.[1]

The economists flatly deny that labor unions and government pro-labor legislation can and did lastingly benefit the whole class of wage earners and raise their standard of living. But the facts, say the anti-economists, have refuted these fallacies. As they see it, the statesmen and legislators who enacted the factory acts displayed a better insight into reality than the economists. While laissez-faire philosophy allegedly taught that the sufferings of the toiling masses are unavoidable, the common sense of laymen succeeded in quelling the worst excesses of profit-seeking business. The improvement in the conditions of the workers, they say, is entirely an achievement of governments and labor unions.

Such are the ideas permeating most of the historical studies dealing with the evolution of modern industrialism. The authors begin by sketching an idyllic image of conditions as they prevailed on the eve of the "Industrial Revolution." At that time, they tell us, things were, by and large, satisfactory. The peasants were happy. So also were the industrial workers under the domestic system. They worked in their own cottages and enjoyed a certain economic independence since they owned a garden plot and their tools. But then "the Industrial Revolution fell like a war or a plague" on these people.[2] The factory system reduced the free worker to virtual slavery; it lowered his standard of

Ludwig von Mises (1881–1973) was one of the great defenders of a rational economic science, and perhaps the single most creative mind at work in this field in our century. This essay, which appeared in the February 1956 issue of *The Freeman*, was adapted from *Human Action* (New Haven: Yale University Press, 1949 [Fourth edition, The Foundation for Economic Education, 1996]), pp. 617–623.

living to the level of bare subsistence; in cramming women and children into the mills it destroyed family life and sapped the very foundations of society, morality, and public health. A small minority of ruthless exploiters had cleverly succeeded in imposing their yoke upon the immense majority.

The truth is that economic conditions were highly unsatisfactory on the eve of the Industrial Revolution. The traditional social system was not elastic enough to provide for the needs of a rapidly increasing population. Neither farming nor the guilds had any use for the additional hands. Business was imbued with the inherited spirit of privilege and exclusive monopoly; its institutional foundations were licenses and the grant of a patent of monopoly; its philosophy was restriction and the prohibition of competition both domestic and foreign. The number of people for whom there was no room left in the rigid system of paternalism and government tutelage of business grew rapidly. They were virtually outcasts. The apathetic majority of these wretched people lived from the crumbs that fell from the tables of the established castes. In the harvest season they earned a trifle by occasional help on farms; for the rest they depended upon private charity and communal poor relief. Thousands of the most vigorous youths of these strata were pressed into the service of the Royal Army and Navy; many of them were killed or maimed in action; many more perished ingloriously from the hardships of the barbarous discipline, from tropical diseases, or from syphilis.[3] Other thousands, the boldest and most ruthless of their class, infested the country as vagabonds, beggars, tramps, robbers, and prostitutes. The authorities did not know of any means to cope with these individuals other than the poorhouse and the workhouse. The support the government gave to the popular resentment against the introduction of new inventions and labor-saving devices made things quite hopeless.

The factory system developed in a continuous struggle against innumerable obstacles. It had to fight popular prejudice, old established customs, legally binding rules and regulations, the animosity of the authorities, the vested interests of privileged groups, the envy of the guilds. The capital equipment of the individual firms was insufficient, the provision of credit extremely difficult and costly. Technological and commercial experience was lacking. Most factory owners failed; comparatively few succeeded. Profits were sometimes considerable, but so were losses. It took many decades until the common practice of reinvesting the greater part of profits earned accumulated adequate capital for the conduct of affairs on a broader scale.

That the factories could thrive in spite of all these hindrances was due to two reasons. First there were the teachings of the new social philosophy expounded by economists, who demolished the prestige of mercantilism, paternalism, and restrictionism. They exploded the superstitious belief that labor-saving devices and processes cause unemployment and reduce all people to poverty and decay. The laissez-faire economists were the pioneers of the unprecedented technological achievements of the last two hundred years.

Then there was another factor that weakened the opposition to innovations. The factories freed the authorities and the ruling landed aristocracy from an embarrassing problem that had grown too large for them. They provided sustenance for the masses of paupers. They emptied the poorhouses, the workhouses, and the prisons. They converted starving beggars into self-supporting breadwinners.

The factory owners did not have the power to compel anybody to take a factory job. They could only hire people who were ready to work for the wages offered to them. Low as these wage rates were, they were nonetheless much more than these paupers could earn in any other field open to them. It is a distortion of facts to say that the factories carried off the housewives from the nurseries and the kitchens and the children from their play. These women had nothing to cook with and to feed their children. These children were destitute and starving. Their only refuge was the factory. It saved them, in the strict sense of the term, from death by starvation.

It is deplorable that such conditions existed. But if one wants to blame those responsible, one must not blame the factory owners who—driven by selfishness, of course, and not by "altruism"—did all they could to eradicate the evils. What had caused these evils was the economic order of the precapitalistic era, the order of the "good old days."

In the first decades of the Industrial Revolution the standard of living of the factory workers was shockingly bad when compared with contemporary conditions of the upper classes and with the present conditions of the industrial masses. Hours of work were long, the sanitary conditions in the workshops deplorable. The individual's capacity to work was used up rapidly. But the fact remains that for the surplus population which the enclosure movement had reduced to dire wretchedness and for which there was literally no room left in the frame of the prevailing system of production, work in the factories was salvation. These people thronged into the plants for no reason other than the urge to improve their standard of living.

The laissez-faire ideology and its offshoot, the "Industrial Revolution," blasted the ideological and institutional barriers to progress and welfare. They demolished the social order in which a constantly increasing number of people were doomed to abject need and destitution. The processing trades of earlier ages had almost exclusively catered to the wants of the well-to-do. Their expansion was limited by the amount of luxuries the wealthier strata of the population could afford. Those not engaged in the production of primary commodities could earn a living only as far as the upper classes were disposed to utilize their skill and services. But now a different principle came into operation. The factory system inaugurated a new mode of marketing as well as of production. Its characteristic feature was that the manufactures were not designed for the consumption of a few well-to-do only, but for the consumption of those who had hitherto played but a negligible role as consumers. Cheap things for the many was the objective of the factory system. The classical factory of the early days of the Industrial Revolution was the cotton mill. Now, the cotton goods it turned out were not something the rich were asking for. These wealthy people clung to silk, linen, and cambric.

Whenever the factory with its methods of mass production by means of power-driven machines invaded a new branch of production, it started with the production of cheap goods for the broad masses. The factories turned to the production of more refined and therefore more expensive goods only at a later stage, when the unprecedented improvement in the masses' standard of living which they caused made it profitable to apply the methods of mass production also to these better articles. Thus, for instance, the factory-made shoe was for many years bought only by the "proletarians" while the wealthier consumers continued to patronize the custom shoemakers. The much-talked-about sweatshops did not produce clothes for the rich, but for people in modest circumstances. The fashionable ladies and gentlemen preferred and still do prefer custom-made frocks and suits.

The outstanding fact about the Industrial Revolution is that it opened an age of mass production for the needs of the masses. The wage earners are no longer people toiling merely for other people's well-being. They themselves are the main consumers of the products the factories turn out. Big business depends upon mass consumption. There is, in present-day America, not a single branch of big business that would not cater to the needs of the masses. The very principle of capitalist entrepreneurship is to provide for the common man. In his capacity as consumer the common man is the sovereign whose buying or abstention from buying decides the fate of entrepreneurial activities. There is in the market economy no other means of acquiring and preserving wealth than by supplying the masses in the best and cheapest way with all the goods they ask for.

Blinded by their prejudices, many historians and writers have entirely failed to recognize this fundamental fact. As they see it, wage earners toil for the benefit of other people. They never raise the question who these "other" people are.

Mr. and Mrs. Hammond tell us that the workers were happier in 1760 than they were in 1830.[4] This is an arbitrary value judgment. There is no means of comparing and measuring the happiness of different people and of the same people at different times. We may agree for the sake of argument that an individual who was born in 1740 was happier in 1760 than in 1830. But let us not forget that in 1770 (according to the estimate of Arthur Young) England had 8.5 million inhabitants, while in 1831 (according to the census) the figure was 16 million.[5] This conspicuous increase was mainly conditioned by the Industrial Revolution. With regard to these additional Englishmen the assertion of the eminent historians can only be approved by those who endorse the melancholy verses of Sophocles: "Not to be born is, beyond all question, the best; but when a man has once seen the light of day, this is next best, that speedily he should return to that place whence he came."

The early industrialists were for the most part men who had their origin in the same social strata from which their workers came. They lived very modestly, spent only a fraction of their earnings for their households, and put the rest back into the business. But as the entrepreneurs grew richer, the sons of successful businessmen began to intrude into the circles of the ruling class. The highborn gentlemen envied the wealth of the parvenus and resented their sympathies with the reform movement. They hit back by investigating the material and moral conditions of the factory hands and enacting factory legislation.

The history of capitalism in Great Britain as well as in all other capitalist countries is a record of an unceasing tendency toward the improvement in the wage earners' standard of living. This evolution coincided with the development of prolabor legislation and the spread of labor unionism on the one hand and with the increase in the marginal productivity of labor on the other hand. The economists assert that the improvement in the workers' material conditions is due to the increase in the per capita quota of capital invested and the technological achievements which the employment of this additional capital brought about. As far as labor legislation and union pressure did not exceed the limits of what the workers would have got without them as a necessary consequence of the acceleration of capital accumulation as compared with population, they were superfluous. As far as they exceeded these limits, they were harmful to the interests of the masses. They delayed the accumulation of capital, thus slowing down the tendency toward a rise in the marginal productivity of labor and in wage rates. They conferred privileges on some groups of wage earners at the expense of other groups. They created mass unemployment and decreased the amount of products available for the workers in their capacity as consumers.

The apologists of government interference with business and of labor unionism ascribe all the improvements in the conditions of the workers to the actions of governments and unions. Except for them, they contend, the workers' standard of living would be no higher today than it was in the early years of the factory system.

It is obvious that this controversy cannot be settled by appeal to historical experience. With regard to the establishment of the facts there is no disagreement between the two groups. Their antagonism concerns the interpretation of events, and this interpretation must be guided by the theory chosen. The epistemological and logical considerations which determine the correctness or incorrectness of a theory are logically and temporarily antecedent to the elucidation of the historical problem involved. The historical facts as such neither prove nor disprove any theory. They need to be interpreted in the light of theoretical insight.

Most of the authors who wrote the history of the conditions of labor under capitalism were ignorant of economics and boasted of this ignorance. However, this contempt for sound economic reasoning did not mean that they approached the topic of their studies without prepossession and without bias in favor of any theory. They were guided by the popular fallacies concerning governmental omnipotence and the alleged blessings of labor unionism. It is beyond question that the Webbs as well as Lujo Brentano and a host of minor authors were at the very start of their studies imbued with a fanatical dislike of the market economy and an enthusiastic endorsement of the doctrines of socialism and interventionism. They were certainly honest and sincere in their convictions and tried to do their best. Their candor and probity exonerates them as individuals; it does not exonerate them as historians. However pure the intentions of a historian may be, there is no excuse for his recourse to fallacious doctrines. The first duty of a historian is to examine with the utmost care all the doctrines to which he resorts in dealing with the subject matter of his work. If he neglects to do this and naively espouses the garbled and confused ideas of popular opinion, he is not a historian but an apologist and propagandist.

The antagonism between the two opposite points of view is not merely a historical problem. It refers no less to the most burning problems of the present day. It is the matter of controversy in what is called in present-day America the problem of industrial relations.

Let us stress one aspect of the matter only. Vast areas—China, the East Indies, Southern and Southeastern Europe, Latin America—are only superficially affected by modern capitalism. Conditions in these countries by and large do not differ from those of England on the eve of the "Industrial Revolution." There are millions and millions of people for whom there is no secure place left in the traditional economic setting. The fate of these wretched masses can be improved only by industrialization. What they need most is entrepreneurs and capitalists. As their own foolish policies have deprived these nations of the further enjoyment of the assistance imported foreign capital hitherto gave them, they must embark upon domestic capital accumulation. They must go through all the stages through which the evolution of Western industrialism had to pass. They must start with comparatively low wage rates and long hours of work. But, deluded by the doctrines prevailing in present-day Western Europe and North America, their statesmen think that they can proceed in a different way. They encourage labor-union pressure and alleged pro-labor legislation. Their interventionist radicalism nips in the bud all attempts to create domestic industries. These men do not comprehend that industrialization cannot begin with the adoption of the precepts of the International Labor Office and the principles of the American Congress of Industrial Organizations. Their stubborn dogmatism spells the doom of the Indian and Chinese coolies, the Mexican peons, and millions of other peoples, desperately struggling on the verge of starvation.

---

1. The attribution of the phrase "the Industrial Revolution" to the reigns of the two last Hanoverian Georges was the outcome of deliberate attempts to melodramatize economic history in order to fit it into the Procrustean Marxian schemes. The transition from medieval methods of production to those of the free enterprise system was a long process that started centuries before 1760 and, even in England, was not finished in 1830. Yet, it is true that England's industrial development was considerably accelerated in the second half of the eighteenth century. It is therefore permissible to use the term "Industrial Revolution" in the examination of the emotional connotations with which Fabianism, Marxism, the Historical School, and Institutionalism have loaded it.

2. J.L. Hammond and Barbara Hammond, *The Skilled Laborer 1760–1832,* 2nd ed. (London, 1920), p. 4.

3. In the Seven Years' War, 1,512 British seamen were killed in battle while 133,708 died of disease or were missing. See W. L. Dorn, *Competition for Empire 1740–1763* (New York, 1940), p. 114.

4. Hammond and Hammond, p. 4.

5. F. C. Dietz, *An Economic History of England* (New York, 1942), pp. 279 and 392.

Child Labor and the British Industrial Revolution

by Lawrence W. Reed

Everyone agrees that in the 100 years between 1750 and 1850 there took place in Great Britain profound economic changes. This was the age of the Industrial Revolution, complete with a cascade of technical innovations, a vast increase in industrial production, a renaissance of world trade, and rapid growth of urban populations.

Where historians and other observers clash is in the interpretation of these great changes. Were they "good" or "bad"? Did they represent improvement to the citizens, or did these events set them back? Perhaps no other issue within this realm has generated more intellectual heat than the one concerning the labor of children. The enemies of freedom—of capitalism—have successfully cast this matter as an irrefutable indictment of the capitalist system as it was emerging in nineteenth-century Britain.

The many reports of poor working conditions and long hours of difficult toil make harrowing reading, to be sure. William Cooke Taylor wrote at the time about contemporary reformers who, witnessing children at work in factories, thought to themselves, "How much more delightful would have been the gambol of the free limbs on the hillside; the sight of the green mead with its spangles of buttercups and daisies; the song of the bird and the humming of the bee."[1]

Of those historians who have interpreted child labor in industrial Britain as a crime of capitalism, none have been more prominent than J.L. and Barbara Hammond. Their many works, including *Lord Shaftesbury* (1923), *The Village Labourer* (1911), *The Town Labourer* (1917), and *The Skilled Labourer* (1919), have been widely promoted as "authoritative" on the issue.

The Hammonds divided the factory children into two classes: "parish apprentice children" and "free labour children." It is a distinction of enormous significance, though one the authors themselves

Mr. Reed, economist and author, is president of the Mackinac Center for Public Policy, a free-market research and educational organization in Midland, Michigan. An earlier version of this essay appeared as a chapter in *Ideas on Liberty: Essays in Honor of Paul L. Poirot*, published by FEE.

failed utterly to appreciate. Once having made the distinction, the Hammonds proceeded to treat the two classes as though no distinction between them existed at all. A deluge of false and misleading conclusions about capitalism and child labor has poured forth for years as a consequence.

Opportunity or Oppression?

"Free labour" children were those who lived at home but worked during the days in factories at the insistence of their parents or guardians. British historian E. P. Thompson, though generally critical of the factory system, nonetheless quite properly conceded that "it is perfectly true that the parents not only needed their children's earnings, but expected them to work."[2]

Professor Ludwig von Mises, the great Austrian economist, put it well when he noted that the generally deplorable conditions extant for centuries before the Industrial Revolution, and the low levels of productivity which created them, *caused* families to embrace the new opportunities the factories represented: "It is a distortion of facts to say that the factories carried off the housewives from the nurseries and the kitchen and the children from their play. These women had nothing to cook with and to feed their children. These children were destitute and starving. Their only refuge was the factory. It saved them, in the strict sense of the term, from death by starvation."[3]

Private factory owners could not forcibly subjugate "free labour" children; they could not compel them to work in conditions their parents found unacceptable. The mass exodus from the socialist Continent to increasingly capitalist, industrial Britain in the first half of the nineteenth century strongly suggests that people did indeed find the industrial order an attractive alternative. And no credible evidence exists that parents in these early capitalist days were any less caring of their offspring than those of pre-capitalist times.

The situation, however, was much different for "parish apprentice" children, and close examination reveals that it was *these* children on whom the critics were focusing when they spoke of the "evils" of capitalism's Industrial Revolution. These youngsters, it turns out, were under the direct authority and supervision *not* of their parents in a free-labor market, but of *government* officials. Most were orphans; a few were victims of negligent parents or parents whose health or lack of skills kept them from earning sufficient income to care for a family. All were in the custody of "parish authorities." As the Hammonds wrote, "the first mills were placed on streams, and the necessary labour was provided by the importation of cartloads of pauper children from the workhouses of the big towns. London was an important source, for since the passing of Hanway's Act in 1767 the child population in the workhouse had enormously increased, and the parish authorities were anxious to find relief from the burden of their maintenance. . . . To the parish authorities, encumbered with great masses of unwanted children, the new cotton mills in Lancashire, Derby, and Notts were a godsend."[4]

The Hammonds proceed to report the horrors of these mills with descriptions like these: "crowded with overworked children," "hotbeds of putrid fever," "monotonous toil in a hell of human cruelty," and so forth. Page after page of the Hammonds' writings—as well as those of many other anti-capitalist historians—deal in this manner with the condition of these parish apprentices. Though consigned to the control of a government authority, these children are routinely held up as victims of the "capitalist order."

Author Robert Hessen is one observer who has taken note of this historiographical mischief and has urged others to acknowledge the error. The parish apprentice children, he writes, "were sent into virtual slavery by *a government body*; they were deserted or orphaned pauper children who were legally under the custody of the poor-law officials in the parish, and who were bound by these officials into long terms of unpaid apprenticeship in return for bare subsistence."[5] Indeed, Hessen points out, the first act in Britain which applied to factory children was passed to protect these very parish apprentices, not "free labour" children.

The Role of the State

It has not been uncommon for historians, including many who lived and wrote in the nineteenth century, to report the travails of the apprentice children without ever realizing they were effectively indicting *government*, not the economic arrangement of free exchange we call capitalism. In 1857, Alfred Kydd published a two-volume work entitled *The History of the Factory Movement*. He speaks of "living bodies caught in the iron grip of machinery in rapid motion, and whirled in the air, bones crushed, and blood cast copiously on the floor, because of physical exhaustion." Then, in a most revealing statement, in which he refers to the children's "owners," Kydd declares that "The factory apprentices have been *sold* [emphasis mine] by auction as 'bankrupt's effects.'"[6]

A surgeon by the name of Philip Gaskell made extensive observations of the physical condition of the manufacturing population in the

1830s. He published his findings in a book in 1836 entitled *Artisans and Machinery*. The casual reader would miss the fact that, in his revelations of ghastly conditions for children, he was referring to the parish apprentices: "That glaring mismanagement existed in numberless instances there can be no doubt; and that these unprotected creatures, thus thrown entirely into the power of the manufacturer, were over-worked, often badly-fed, and worse treated. No wonder can be felt that these glaring mischiefs attracted observation, and finally, led to the passing of the Apprentice Bill, a bill intended to regulate these matters."[7]

The Apprentice Bill that Gaskell mentioned was passed in 1802, the first of the much-heralded factory legislation, the very one Hessen stresses was aimed at the abuse by the parish officials. It remains that capitalism is not a system of compulsion. The lack of physical force, in fact, is what distinguishes it from pre-capitalist, feudal times. When feudalism reigned, men, women, and children were indeed "sold" at auction, forced to work long hours at arduous manual labor, and compelled to toil under whatever conditions and for whatever compensation pleased their masters. This was the system of serfdom, and the deplorable system of parish apprenticeship was a remnant of Britain's feudal past.

The emergence of capitalism was sparked by a desire of Englishmen to rid themselves of coercive economic arrangements. The free laborer increasingly supplanted the serf as capitalism blossomed. It is a gross and most unfortunate distortion of history for anyone to contend that capitalism or its industrialization was to blame for the agony of the apprentice children.

Though it is inaccurate to judge capitalism guilty of the sins of parish apprenticeship, it would also be inaccurate to assume that free-labor children worked under ideal conditions in the early days of the Industrial Revolution. By today's standards, their situation was clearly bad. Such capitalist achievements as air conditioning and high levels of productivity would, in time, substantially ameliorate it, however. The evidence in favor of capitalism is thus compellingly suggestive: From 1750 to 1850, when the population of Great Britain nearly tripled, *the exclusive choice* of those flocking to the country for jobs was to work for private capitalists.

The Sadler Report

A discussion of child labor in Britain would be incomplete without some reference to the famous Sadler Report. Written by a member of

Parliament in 1832 and filled with stories of brutality, degradation, and oppression against factory workers of all ages and status, it became the bible for indignant reformers well into the twentieth century. The Hammonds described it as "one of the main sources of our knowledge of the conditions of factory life at the time. Its pages bring before the reader in vivid form of dialogue the kind of life that was led by the victims of the new system."[8] Two other historians, B.L. Hutchins and A. Harrison, describe it as "one of the most valuable collections of evidence on industrial conditions that we possess."[9]

W.H. Hutt, in his essay, "The Factory System of the Early Nineteenth Century," reveals that bad as things were, they were never nearly as bad as the Sadler Report would have one believe. Sadler, it turns out, had been agitating for passage of the Ten Hours' Bill, and in doing so he employed every cheap political trick in the book, including the falsification of evidence.[10] The report was part of those tactics.

Hutt quotes R.H. Greg (author of *The Factory Question*, 1837), who accused Sadler of giving to the world "such a mass of *ex-parte* statements, and of gross falsehoods and calumnies . . . as probably never before found their way into any public document."[11]

This view is shared by no less an anticapitalist than Friedrich Engels, partner of Karl Marx. In his book, *The Condition of the Working Class in England*, Engels says this of the Sadler Report: "This is a very partisan document, which was drawn up entirely by enemies of the factory system for purely political purposes. Sadler was led astray by his passionate sympathies into making assertions of a most misleading and erroneous kind. He asked witnesses questions in such a way as to elicit answers which, although correct, nevertheless were stated in such a form as to give a wholly false impression."[12]

As already explained, the first of the factory legislation was an act of mercy for the enslaved apprentice children. Successive acts between 1819 and 1846, however, placed greater and greater restrictions on the employment of free-labor children. Were they necessary to correct alleged "evils of industrialization"?

The evidence strongly suggests that whatever benefits the legislation may have produced by preventing children from going to work (or raising the cost of employing them) were marginal, and probably were outweighed by the harm the laws actually caused. Gaskell admitted a short time after one of them had passed that it "caused multitudes of children to be dismissed, but it has only increased the evils it was intended to remedy, and must of necessity be repealed."[13]

Hutt believes that "in the case of children's labor, the effects (of restrictive laws) went further than the mere loss of their work; they lost their training and, consequently, their skill as adults."[14]

Conditions of employment and sanitation were best, as the Factory Commission of 1833 documented, in the larger and newer factories. The owners of these larger establishments, which were more easily and frequently subject to visitation and scrutiny by inspectors, increasingly chose to dismiss children from employment rather than be subjected to elaborate, arbitrary, and ever-changing rules on how they might run a factory employing youths. The result of legislative intervention was that these dismissed children, most of whom needed to work in order to survive, were forced to seek jobs in smaller, older, and more out-of-the-way places where sanitation, lighting, and safety were markedly inferior.[15] Those who could not find new jobs were reduced to the status of their counterparts a hundred years before, that is, to irregular and grueling agricultural labor, or worse—in the words of Mises—"infested the country as vagabonds, beggars, tramps, robbers, and prostitutes."[16]

So it is that child labor was relieved of its worst attributes not by legislative fiat, but by the progressive march of an ever more productive, capitalist system. Child labor was virtually eliminated when, for the first time in history, the productivity of parents in free labor markets rose to the point that it was no longer economically necessary for children to work in order to survive. The emancipators and benefactors of children were not legislators or factory inspectors, but factory owners and financiers. Their efforts and investments in machinery led to a rise in real wages, to a growing abundance of goods at lower prices, and to an incomparable improvement in the general standard of living.

Of all the interpretations of industrial history, it would be difficult to find one more perverse than that which ascribes the suffering of children to capitalism and its Industrial Revolution. The popular critique of child labor in industrial Britain is unwarranted, misdirected propaganda. The Hammonds and others should have focused on the activities of *government*, not capitalists, as the source of the children's plight. It is a confusion which has unnecessarily taken a heavy toll on the case for freedom and free markets. On this issue, it is long overdue for the friends of capitalism to take the ideological and historiographical offensive.

---

1. William Cooke Taylor, *The Factory System* (London, 1844), pp. 23–24.

2. E. P. Thompson, *The Making of the English Working Class* (New York: Random House, 1964), p. 339.

3. Ludwig von Mises, *Human Action* (New Haven, Conn.: Yale University Press, 1949), p. 615.

4. J.L. Hammond and Barbara Hammond, *The Town Labourer* (New York: Augustus M. Kelley, 1967), p. 145.

5. Robert Hessen, "The Effects of the Industrial Revolution on Women and Children," in Ayn Rand, *Capitalism: The Unknown Ideal* (New York: New American Library, 1967), p. 112.

6. Alfred Kydd, *The History of the Factory Movement* (New York: Burt Franklin, n.d.), pp. 21–22.

7. Philip Gaskell, *Artisans and Machinery* (New York: Augustus M. Kelley, 1968), p. 141.

8. J.L.Hammond and Barbara Hammond, *Lord Shaftesbury* (London: Constable, 1933), p. 16.

9. B.L. Hutchins and A. Harrison, *A History of Factory Legislation* (New York: Augustus M. Kelley, 1966), p. 34.

10. W.H. Hutt, "The Factory System of the Early Nineteenth Century," in F.A. Hayek, *Capitalism and the Historians* (Chicago: University of Chicago Press, 1954), p. 1.

11. Hutt, p. 1.

12. Friedrich Engels, *The Condition of the Working Class in England* (New York: Macmillan, 1958), p. 192.

13. Gaskell, p. 67.

14. Hutt, p. 182.

15. Hessen, p. 112.

16. Mises, p. 614.

Economic Myths of Early Capitalism

by F. A. Hayek

There is one supreme myth which more than any other has served to discredit the economic system to which we owe our present-day civilization. It is the legend of the deterioration of the position of the working classes in consequence of the rise of "capitalism" (or of the "manufacturing" or the "industrial system").

Who has not heard of the "horrors of early capitalism" and gained the impression that the advent of this system brought untold new suffering to large classes who before were tolerably content and comfortable? We might justly hold in disrepute a system to which the blame attached that even for a time it worsened the position of the poorest and most numerous class of the population. The widespread emotional aversion to "capitalism" is closely connected with this belief that the undeniable growth of wealth which the competitive order has produced was purchased at the price of depressing the standard of life of the weakest elements of society.

That this was the case was at one time indeed widely taught by economic historians. A more careful examination of the facts has, however, led to a thorough refutation of this belief. Yet, a generation after the controversy has been decided, popular opinion still continues as though the older belief had been true.

False Interpretation

Discussions of the effects of the rise of modern industry on the working classes refer almost always to the conditions in England in the first half of the nineteenth century; yet the great change to which they refer had commenced much earlier, and by then had quite a long history and had spread far beyond England. The freedom of economic activity which in England had proved so favorable to the rapid growth of wealth was probably in the first instance an almost accidental by-product of the limitations which the revolution of the seventeenth century had placed on the powers of government; and only after its bene-

Dr. F. A. Hayek (1899–1992), a disciple of Ludwig von Mises, and one of the seminal thinkers of the twentieth century, was the author of such classics as *The Road to Serfdom* and *The Constitution of Liberty*. He won the Nobel Prize for Economics in 1974. This article was published in FEE's *Essays on Liberty*, Vol. III, in 1958.

ficial effects had come to be widely noticed did the economists later undertake to explain the connection and to argue for the removal of the remaining barriers to commercial freedom. In many ways it is misleading to speak of "capitalism" as though this had been a new and altogether different system which suddenly came into being toward the end of the eighteenth century; we use this term here because it is the most familiar name, but only with great reluctance, since with its modern connotations it is itself largely a creation of that socialist interpretation of economic history with which we are concerned. The term is especially misleading when, as is often the case, it is connected with the idea of the rise of the propertyless proletariat, which by some devious process have been deprived of their rightful ownership of the tools for their work.

Survival

The actual history of the connection between capitalism and the rise of the proletariat is almost the opposite of that which these theories of the expropriation of the masses suggest. The truth is that, for the greater part of history, for most men the possession of the tools for their work was an essential condition for survival or at least for being able to rear a family.

The number of those who could maintain themselves by working for others, although they did not themselves possess the necessary equipment, was limited to a small proportion of the population. The amount of arable land and of tools handed down from one generation to the next limited the total number who could survive. To be left without them meant in most instances death by starvation or at least the impossibility of procreation. There was little incentive and little possibility for one generation to accumulate the additional tools which would have made possible the survival of a larger number of the next, so long as the advantage of employing additional hands was limited mainly to the instances where the division of the tasks increased the efficiency of the work of the owner of the tools.

It was only when the larger gains from the employment of machinery provided both the means and the opportunity for their investment what in the past had been a recurring surplus of population doomed to early death was in an increasing measure given the possibility of survival. Numbers which had been practically stationary for many centuries began to increase rapidly. The proletariat which capitalism can be said to have "created" was thus not a proportion of the population which would have existed without it and which it had degraded to a lower level; it was an additional population which was enabled to grow up by the new opportunities for employment which capitalism provided.

Rise of Modern Industry

Insofar as it is true that the growth of capital made the appearance of the proletariat possible, it was in the sense that it raised the productivity of labor, so that much larger numbers of those who had not been equipped by their parents with the necessary tools were enabled to maintain themselves by their labor alone; but the capital had to be supplied first before those were enabled to survive who afterward claimed as a right a share in its ownership.

Although it was certainly not from charitable motives, it still was the first time in history that one group of people found it in their interest to use their earnings on a large scale to provide new instruments of production to be operated by those who without them could not have produced their own sustenance.

Of the effect of the rise of modern industry on the growth of population, statistics tell a vivid tale. That this in itself largely contradicts the common belief about the harmful effect of the rise of the factory system on the large masses is not the point with which we are at present concerned. Nor need we more than mention the fact that, so long as this increase of the numbers of those whose output reached a certain level brought forward a fully corresponding increase in population, the level of the poorest fringe could not be substantially improved, however much the average might rise. The point of immediate relevance is that this increase of population and particularly of the manufacturing population had proceeded in England at least for two or three generations before the period of which it is alleged that the position of the workers seriously deteriorated.

The period to which this refers is also the period when the problem of the position of the working class became for the first time one of general concern. And the opinions of some of the contemporaries are indeed the main source of the present beliefs. Our first question must therefore be how it came about that such an impression contrary to the facts should have become widely held among the people then living.

Social Conscience

One of the chief reasons was evidently an increasing awareness of facts which before had passed unnoticed. The very increase of wealth and well-being which had been achieved raised standards and aspirations. What for ages seemed a natural and inevitable situation, or even as an improvement upon the past, came to be regarded as incongruous with the opportunities which the new age appeared to offer. Economic suffering both became conspicuous and seemed less justified because general wealth was increasing faster than ever before. But this, of course, does not prove that the people whose fate was beginning to cause indignation and alarm were worse off than their parents or grandparents had been. While there is every evidence that great misery existed, there is none that it was greater than or even as great as it had been before.

The aggregations of large numbers of cheap houses of industrial workers were probably more ugly than the picturesque cottages in which some of the agricultural laborers or domestic workers had lived; and they were certainly more alarming to the landowner or to the city patrician than the poor dispersed over the country had been. But for those who had moved from country to town it meant an improvement; and even though the rapid growth of the industrial centers created sanitary problems with which people had yet slowly and painfully to learn to cope, statistics leave little doubt that even general health was on the whole benefited rather than harmed.

More important, however, for the explanation of the change from an optimistic to a pessimistic view of the effects of industrialization than this awakening of social conscience was probably the fact that this change of opinion appears to have commenced, not in the manufacturing districts which had firsthand knowledge of what was happening, but in the political discussion of the English metropolis which was somewhat remote from, and had little part in, the new development.

It is evident that the belief about the "horrible" conditions prevailing among the manufacturing populations of the Midlands and the north of England was in the 1830s and 1840s widely held among the upper classes of London and the south. It was one of the main arguments with which the landowning class hit back at the manufacturers to counter the agitation of the latter against the Corn Laws and for free trade. And it was from these arguments of the conservative press that the radical intelligentsia of the time, with little firsthand knowledge of the industrial districts, derived their views which were to become the standard weapons of political propaganda.

Labor Displacement Fallacy

It may seem obvious that the introduction of machinery will produce a general reduction of the demand for labor. But persistent effort to think the problem through shows that this belief is the result of a logical fallacy, of stressing one effect of the assumed change and leaving out others. Nor do the facts give any support to the belief. Yet anyone who thinks it to be true is very likely to find what seems to him confirming evidence. It is easy enough to find the early nineteenth-century instances of extreme poverty and to draw the conclusion that this must have been the effect of the introduction of machinery, without asking whether conditions had been any better or perhaps even worse before. Or one may believe that an increase of production must lead to the impossibility of selling all the product; and when one then finds a stagnation of sales, regard this as a confirmation of the expectations, although there are several more plausible explanations than general "overproduction" or "underconsumption."

There can be no doubt that many of these misrepresentations were put forward in good faith; and there is no reason why we should not respect the motives of some of those who, to arouse public conscience, painted the misery of the poor in the blackest colors. We owe to agitation of this kind, which forced unwilling eyes to face unpleasant facts, some of the finest and most generous acts of public policy—from the abolition of slavery to the removal of taxes on imported food and the destruction of many intrenched monopolies and abuses. And there is every reason to remember how miserable the majority of the people still were as recently as a hundred or a hundred and fifty years ago.

But we must not, long after the event, allow a distortion of the facts, even if committed out of humanitarian zeal, to affect our view of what we owe to a system which for the first time in history made people feel that this misery might be avoidable. The very claims and ambitions of the working classes were and are the result of the enormous improvement of their position which capitalism brought about.

A Christian Speaks Up for Capitalism

by James D. Gwartney

Many Christian leaders—evangelical, mainline Protestant, and Roman Catholic—appear to have a feeling that capitalism is unfair and needs more government intervention to keep it humane. While many of us who are both Christians and economists consider this view misguided, we sometimes lack arguments to help change this view. I'd like to offer a few.

What I am defending when I speak of capitalism is a social order that provides for the protection of one's possessions as long as they are acquired without the use of violence, theft, or fraud; and that relies primarily on free-market prices to allocate goods and services—the fundamental social system of the United States. Here are some reasons why Christians might think more charitably about it:

Capitalism rewards and reinforces service to others. Under capitalism, a person's income is directly related to his or her ability to provide goods and services that enhance the welfare of others. Business winners are those who figure out what customers want and offer them a better deal than they can get elsewhere.

Moreover, such enterprises put pressure on other businesses to serve customers better—as you know if you have observed how retailers respond to the opening of a new discount store. Of course, people in business do not have to care about other people, as Christians are directed to do. But if they want to succeed, they must serve their customers better than the competition. In essence, competition forces business people to act *as if* they care about others.

Capitalism provides for the masses, not just the elite. To succeed in a big way under capitalism, you have to produce something that appeals to many people. Henry Ford became a multimillionaire by bringing a low-cost automobile within the budget of mass consumers. In contrast, Sir Henry Royce, died a man of modest wealth. He engi-

---

Dr. Gwartney is professor of economics at Florida State University. This article was originally published in the August 1986 issue of *The Freeman*.

neered a far superior car to Ford, the Rolls Royce, but he designed it for the rich. The market rewarded him accordingly.

Capitalism provides opportunity for achievers of all socio-economic backgrounds to move up the economic ladder. It is no coincidence that poor people around the world flow toward capitalist countries rather than away from them. Poor Mexican laborers risk their lives for work opportunities in the United States. In Europe, the Soviets built a wall to keep people from the capitalist West. In Southeast Asia, people are drawn to Hong Kong, Taiwan, Thailand, and other capitalist countries. Why? Because capitalism provides opportunity for those who want to achieve.

In the United States, previously poverty-stricken refugees are succeeding as restaurant operators, taxicab drivers, and business entrepreneurs. A recent study found that nearly half of the families in the bottom one-fifth of the United States income distribution in 1971 made significant moves up the income ladder by 1978. No other system provides more opportunity for advancement, with fewer built-in social rigidities.

Downward movement takes place, too: Riches today do not guarantee success tomorrow. Like the God of Christianity, capitalism is "no respecter of persons."

Capitalism provides for minority views. When decisions are made politically, minority views are often suppressed. For example, in a public school system the political majority decides whether prayer will be allowed, whether sex education will be taught, and how much emphasis to give to basic skills. Those who do not like the decision must either give in or pay for education twice, once as a taxpayer and once in the form of private tuition.

A market system would allow each minority to get its way. For example, without interfering with others' freedom, some parents could send their children to schools that allow prayer. Committed Christians, who often find themselves in the minority, should appreciate this aspect of capitalism, which permits people to pursue divergent goals without conflict or rancor.

Even those who accept these strengths may still feel that capitalism is too materialistic. It is true that this system enables people to attain prosperity, and some people get caught up in the pursuit of wealth. But capitalism does not force individuals to worship "the almighty dollar." A person is as free to be an ascetic Christian as to be a hedonist.

Christians sometimes argue that capitalism promotes inequality, working to the advantage of the rich. Yet inequality is present under all economic systems. The people with better ideas, more creative minds, and more energy will tend to rise to the top in a socialist bureaucracy just as they will in a capitalistic system.

However, elites in a capitalistic system actually have less power than elites in a system where the government predominates. Even in a democracy, elected officials have more power over the lives of others than the wealthiest individuals do. Members of Congress have the power to take a portion of our earnings without our consent, something that David Rockefeller or the Hunt brothers cannot do, no matter how rich they are. Furthermore, if wealthy individuals use their wealth unproductively—that is, for consumption rather than investment or to supply things other people reject—their wealth will shrink over time. Even a "fat cat" living off stock dividends receives those dividends only if the business provides things that people want.

Of course, capitalism does not impose the moral demands that Christianity does. But economic systems seeking to perfect human nature have more often led to tyranny than to bettering the human race. Christians would do well to settle for an economic system that reinforces Christian virtues, improves living standards, and provides for minority views. Capitalism is such a system.

How Capitalism Saved the Whales

by James S. Robbins

It is an article of faith among environmentalists that the ills of the world can be traced to economic and technological development, especially since the Industrial Revolution. The changes that took place in the late eighteenth and early nineteenth centuries, such as harnessing new sources of energy (moving from water to coal power, for example), the development of the factory system, and the human population explosion, they say, led directly to the current problems with waste disposal, air and water pollution, overcrowding, and misused resources, not to mention global warming, ozone depletion, acid rain, and other highly speculative developments.

Fixation on doomsaying can cause environmentalists to forget that the negative consequences of industrialization are minute compared to the positive developments of the industrial age. People are healthier, live longer, and are more productive than ever before in history. But defenders of industrialism can go even further to show that in many cases technological progress has benefited the environment. This is vividly demonstrated in the case of one of the most emotion-laden symbols of environmentalism, the whales.

At the dawn of the industrial age, whales were an important natural resource that humans had been exploiting for centuries. Whales were especially valued for their oil, which was used primarily as fuel for lamps. It was also used for heating, for lubrication, soap, paint, and varnish manufacturing, and the processing of textiles and rope. The Japanese among others had long acquired a taste for whale meat. Regular whale oil ("train oil") was extracted from the blubber which encased the whale's body. But the best oil was spermaceti, found only in the nose of the sperm whale. If exposed to air it would congeal, and was used for smokeless candles, regarded as the finest quality candles ever made.

The sperm whale also sometimes produced ambergris, a sticky substance from the intestines used in the manufacture of perfume.

Mr. Robbins, who has a Ph.D. from the Fletcher School of Law and Diplomacy, is a Contributing Editor of *Liberty* magazine and has written for *The Wall Street Journal*. This article was originally published in the August 1992 issue of *The Freeman*.

Baleen, the bony, plankton-straining ribs in the mouths of most whales (excepting the sperm whale), was lightweight and had good tensile qualities. It was used for a variety of things, including corset stays, umbrella ribs, fishing rods, buggy whips, carriage springs, and skirt hoops. Bones from the body were generally used as fertilizer.

Whaling was a major industry in the nineteenth century, and the United States was the preeminent whaling nation. According to tradition, American commercial whaling began in 1712 in New England. Whaling expanded through the eighteenth century, but was disrupted by the American Revolution and the Napoleonic Wars. In 1815 came peace and rapid growth in the industry. By 1833 there were 392 American whaling vessels. By 1846 there were 735 whalers, comprising 80 percent of the whaling fleet of the entire world. Each year whaling produced 4–5 million gallons of sperm oil, 6–10 million gallons of train oil, and 1.6–5.6 million pounds of bone. The price of train oil rose from 35 cents per gallon in 1825 to 95 cents in 1855.

Though large, whaling was not a robust industry. Even with rising prices, profit margins were always slim, and one in ten ships typically lost money on a voyage. In 1858, a very poor year, 64 percent failed to make a profit. But whalers could always count on an increasing demand for their products, as populations grew and markets expanded accordingly. Had the whaling industry matched the 300 percent population growth from 1850 to 1900, many species of whale would have been extinct long ago.

The Role of Technology in Saving the Whales

Yet, the American whaling industry peaked in the 1850s. The reason for its decline was not because of public awareness of the evils of whaling, it was not because of consciousness-raising efforts by pioneer environmentalists, and it definitely was not because of legislation. The whales were saved because of the march of technology.

The first step that led to saving the whales was made by Dr. Abraham Gesner, a Canadian geologist. In 1849, he devised a method whereby kerosene could be distilled from petroleum. Petroleum had previously been considered either a nuisance, or a miracle cure (an idea originating with Native Americans). Earlier coal-gas methods had been used for lighting since the 1820s, but they were prohibitively expensive. Gesner's kerosene was cheap, easy to produce, could be burned in existing lamps, and did not produce an offensive odor as did most whale oil. It could be stored indefinitely, unlike whale oil, which would eventually spoil. The American petroleum boom began in the 1850s. By the end of the decade there were 30 kerosene plants operating in the United States. The cheaper, more efficient fuel began to drive whale oil out of the market.

The man most responsible for the commercial success of kerosene was John D. Rockefeller. In 1865, at the age of 25, he went into partnership with Samuel Andrews, the part-owner of a Cleveland refinery. Rockefeller had sensed that too much capital was being invested in finding and extracting oil, and not enough was being invested in its processing. Backed by investors, he set up a network of kerosene distilleries that would later develop into Standard Oil.

As kerosene became generally available throughout the country, the demand for whale oil dropped precipitously. The 735-ship fleet of 1846 had shrunk to 39 by 1876. The price of sperm oil reached its high of $1.77 per gallon in 1856; by 1896 it sold for 40 cents. Yet it could not keep pace with the price of refined petroleum, which dropped from 59 cents per gallon in 1865 to a fraction over seven cents in 1895.

Rockefeller, too, would eventually find himself having to adapt to the changing market. A new invention soon snuffed out both flame-based lighting systems. In 1879 Thomas A. Edison began marketing the incandescent light bulb he had invented the previous year. Arc-light technologies had existed since the turn of the century, but it was Edison who devised the modern, commercially feasible light bulb, which produced an even light, burned longer and brighter than oil or kerosene, and was much safer than an open flame. As the country was electrified, whale oil and kerosene were both driven from the illumination market.

American whaling might have expired then, but for the vagaries of fashion. The peripheral market in baleen and whalebone suddenly exploded as more women began to wear corsets, bustles, and other garments that relied for their shape upon the pliant material. From 32 cents per pound in 1870, whalebone rose to $1.12 in 1875, and $3.25 in 1878, reaching $5.00 at the turn of the century. Whalebone constituted 80 percent of the value of a bowhead—sperm whales were given a respite because of their lack of baleen. But by 1908, this market crashed as well. Spring steel replaced whalebone in women's fashions, and as automobiles supplanted horse-drawn carriages, demand for whalebone buggy whips and wagon suspensions collapsed. A few American whalers stayed in business, but their time had passed. The last American whaler left port in 1924, and grounded on Cuttyhunk Island the next day.[1]

Stopping technology in its tracks in the 1850s would have doomed the whales. But suppose whaling had been outlawed then, as it is now? The immediate effect would have been a dramatic decline in quality of life. Would kerosene and electric lamps have come on the scene any faster, in reaction to the sudden surge in demand for substitutes? Maybe—but at the cost of the spirit of innovation which brought the inventions on the scene in the first place. A government that can squelch one endeavor, such as whaling, can outlaw any enterprise. The unpredictability and capriciousness of the state is the true enemy of innovation. Gesner, Rockefeller, and Edison had no intention of saving the whales. Their primary motivation was to make a profit. If the government fosters an atmosphere in which innovation and profit-making potential are subject to whims of bureaucrats, lawyers, and politicians, and not based in the abilities of creative people to find innovative solutions to public needs, innovators will not set their minds to the task, and no state whip can force them to do so. In its time, killing whales was rational, goal-oriented activity, fulfilling human needs. It was not "mindless slaughter" for fun or sport. And the decline of whaling was also rational; human needs remained, even increased—but human ingenuity had found better ways to meet those needs. The whale industry declined—not because of concern for the whales, not because of legislation, but because they were no longer a necessary resource.

The whales were not the only beneficiaries of the technological advancements of the nineteenth century. The Galapagos tortoise was driven almost to extinction because the islands were in the center of a major whaling area, and sailors killed the tortoises for fresh meat. In northern climes, whalers sometimes killed blubber-rich Arctic seals to augment their oil stores. Both of these animals were saved by the decline of whaling. Oil-drilling in Pennsylvania restored many lakes which had been contaminated by natural petroleum leaks. These were all unintended consequences; but the fact that technological development under capitalism manages to produce such consequences consistently argues in favor of the system.

Humans are problem solvers, and the human mind should not be prevented from doing what only it can do. Creative solutions are superior to state restrictions because they strike at the causes of problems, not their effects. Furthermore, just as creative action produces unintentional positive consequences, restricting innovation multiplies negative effects. No one, especially government agencies or neo-Luddites, can anticipate the indirect or unintended favorable consequences of technological innovation. This is why Abraham Gesner, John D. Rockefeller, and Thomas Edison saved more whales than Greenpeace ever will.

---

1. Despite the extinction of American whaling, the whales were not yet safe. The whaling mantle passed to other countries, notably Norway, Japan, and the Soviet Union. Critics of technological development can point to other inventions that kept whaling on

the margins of profitability, notably the rocket harpoon, and the harpoon cannon. The process of hydrogenation gave whale oil new markets in soap and margarine. A by-product of whale oil is glycerine, used in manufacturing explosives, and the two world wars guaranteed a market. The Japanese took increasing numbers of whales for food, and the Soviets used them for animal fodder and fertilizer. By the middle of the twentieth century, whaling had revived.

The second cycle of whaling was more destructive than the first in absolute number; but it never equaled the per capita whale consumption of the previous century. Had per capita rates of the 1850s continued unabated, the total would have been three times that number in the American market alone.

The situation would have been worse for less numerous species. In the first two decades of the nineteenth century, American whalers killed right whales at an average of almost 15,000 per year. When whaling dropped off at the end of the century, there were only about 50,000 right whales left alive.

The Rise of Markets and the Fall of Infectious Disease

by Stephen Gold

My grandmother was deaf, a fact I got used to early in life, but something to which she never fully adjusted. Born with the ability to hear, she lost it in her teens to scarlet fever. The fact that I was unfamiliar with this affliction was of no surprise—most of the serious illnesses my grandmother talked about were foreign to me. The free enterprise system had wiped them out before I was born.

My birth followed my grandmother's by only six decades, a mere blink of an eye in the annals of history. Yet in that brief time civilization had changed more than in all previous centuries combined, mainly through the evolution and expansion of capitalism. Political leaders first recognized the value of free trade and open markets in the 1700s. The concept spread steadily in the 1800s, until by the turn of the century much of the world—most of Europe and North America, as well as the colonies of the far-reaching British Empire—had adopted market economies.

Those countries that opted to remove government controls over the economy and allow private enterprise to flourish saw their citizens grow more affluent. More money meant higher living standards through scientific and technological advances, better nutrition and medicine, and better products and services that were more readily available to the public.

More than anything else, increased wealth brought people increased health.

There's no better example of this than the dramatic reduction in deaths from infectious disease in Western society. It's a David-and-Goliath story, a tale of how one portion of mankind came face to face with its most formidable enemy, and—using newfound knowledge and skills—vanquished its terrifying foe.

And yet, success came so quickly and thoroughly in this battle that most contemporary Americans don't realize how very serious the threat once was. Even with the emergence of AIDS, younger genera-

---

Mr. Gold is director of communications at the Tax Foundation. This article was originally published in the November 1992 issue of *The Freeman*.

tions of Americans do not fear communicable diseases the way their ancestors did. They take for granted the environmental and health gains we have made this century—and forget how these came about. Sadly, having won the battle so efficiently, we have lost perspective on how America got from *there* to *here* in such a short span of time.

It wasn't too long ago that Americans, like so many others around the world, were caught up in a lifelong struggle with such terrifying but familiar contagions as diphtheria, tuberculosis, and typhoid fever. In fact, infectious disease has long been the scourge of human civilization. These restive viruses, bacteria, and protozoa often travel in contaminated water or droplets of saliva, grow on spoiled food, or hitch a ride on parasites like fleas and lice. They thrive in crowded living conditions and filth, and can generally be found in poorer societies that cannot afford the luxury of a cleaner, healthier lifestyle. Each year, for example, 900 million people in underdeveloped countries contract diarrheal diseases stemming from contaminated water and inadequate sanitation.[1]

Historically, the most devastating communicable diseases were plague, smallpox, and typhus. In the almost 3,000 years from the Trojan War to World War I, those infectious diseases claimed probably hundreds of millions of lives worldwide. Fortunately for my grandmother, by the time she was born in 1896 most Americans did not have to deal with these afflictions. The United States had already made significant advances in health and environmental protection, especially as compared to the impoverished nations of South America, Africa, and Asia. Average life expectancy was about 40 percent longer in America than in those preindustrial societies, and pandemic outbreaks were virtually unknown here.[2]

Even so, the United States at the turn of the century—far from being the simple, rustic country envisioned by Americans today—was in fact a nation under siege by infectious diseases. In 1900 over 500 Americans out of every 100,000 died from them, or the often inevitable complications resulting from such illnesses.[3] To put this kind of health threat into perspective, cancer, the scourge of modern America, kills about 200 of every 100,000 Americans each year.[4]

Influenza

As the nineteenth century yielded to the twentieth, America's top killer after heart disease was influenza and its companion, pneumonia. Back then prevention and treatment techniques for such illnesses were still in their infancy. As a result, in 1900 over 200 Americans out of every

100,000—more than 150,000 people—died from influenza or a subsequent case of pneumonia.[5]

The medical record got worse before it got better. In 1918, the final year of World War I, a flu epidemic claimed 550,000 lives in America, 30 million worldwide—three times the number that died in combat in four years of war.[6] Even today, the flu is nothing to sneeze at. About 30 out of every 100,000 Americans, primarily elderly, die from flu complications annually.[7] Still, influenza no longer represents the risk that it once did in our society.

How did we conquer such a devastating illness? Unlike most other communicable diseases, influenza is not associated as much with filth and overcrowding as with a lack of good medical care. Of course, modern medicine is as much a part of the free enterprise story as clean water, adequate sanitation, and improved nutrition. True, much of the foundation for our medical achievements may be traced to the work of dedicated scientists and mathematicians in the preindustrial age. But it took far more than just brilliant minds to produce a healthier population.

In free-market societies, a scientific discovery usually results in competition by entrepreneurs, producers, and doctors to make a profit from a marketable item. In such an atmosphere, each new discovery usually leads to an advance in technology, and ultimately to a new product or service for consumers.

In the battle against flu symptoms, this competitive process led to the development of antipyretics to reduce fever and analgesics to reduce aches and pains. Aspirin, developed near the turn of the century, was both, and as such was considered a miracle cure. Had it somehow been invented in the preindustrial era, only one company would have been licensed to produce it, and only the rich would have had access to it. But in our market economy, numerous companies competed to get the drug into as many hands as possible. That meant coming up with less expensive ways to manufacture and sell it.

When it turned out aspirin was too acidic for some people's stomachs, researchers turned their attention to developing a more soothing medicine. The result, acetaminophen, is used in hospitals nationwide under the brand name Tylenol. Most recently an even stronger analgesic, ibuprofen, has become popular with consumers.

Man versus Mycobacterium

After influenza, tuberculosis was the next great environmental threat to Americans at the century's turn. The germ *Mycobacterium tuberculosis* is sometimes associated with poor hygiene—a social stigma for many turn-of-the-century Americans, a fact of life in much of the rest of the world, even today. Back then TB was also known as "consumption," a telling description of the suffering it caused its victims. Another strain, usually transmitted to children through raw cow's milk, was in past centuries a cause of severe deformities. In all, TB claimed about 2 of every 1,000 American lives in 1900.[8]

The only effective treatment for turn-of-the-century Americans (aside from removing the infected lung) was bed rest, sometimes years of it. In fact, "TB farms" used to dot the countryside, isolating the sick from the rest of the population.

Fortunately, the rise of capitalism provided us with an assortment of tools with which to detect and fight *Mycobacterium tuberculosis.*

For starters, Louis Pasteur's mid-nineteenth-century research on bacteria led other researchers to develop a sterilization process for milk that kills the TB germ. But to market such a product, even regionally, would take special equipment that could heat large quantities of milk to 145 degrees Fahrenheit, then rapidly cool it to below 50 degrees. Then the milk would have to be stored at low temperatures, even during transportation. Who would want to invest the capital and manpower in the search for such technology?

The dairy farmers, of course. The fact that they were motivated by profits rather than philanthropy spurred them to action even more. A larger share of the market could be captured if they sold a safer product. There was some risk: Would consumers want to pay higher prices for the extra service? In this case, the answer was clearly yes. Consumers and health officials alike clamored for germ-free milk, and dairies purchased the necessary machinery and started "pasteurizing" their products.

Competition led other dairies to follow suit. The sterilization process was improved upon and made more efficient, making the product even more affordable. Today, of course, pasteurized milk is sold nationwide.

Other medical advancements, such as the development of vaccines, antibiotics, and x-rays, were equally important in the battle against tuberculosis. It took a combination of thorough research, entrepreneurial spirit, easy access to information, and money to develop all of these, conditions readily available through the freedom and economic incentives of our market economy.

From 1955 to 1985, tuberculosis declined to insignificance. Unfortunately, the United States has since seen a rise in the number of TB cases, mostly in large urban areas and at least partly as a result of the spread of AIDS. Yet to most Americans the threat of tuberculosis is still so remote—fewer than one out of every 100,000 dies from it[9]—that the term "TB farm" would, for today's youth, more likely conjure up images of a diet facility than a rest home.[10]

Conquering Other Health Threats

Diphtheria and typhoid fever, caused by roving bacteria, were also among the greatest public health threats in 1900. Together they claimed 55,000 American lives, more than were killed in car accidents in the United States last year.

Diphtheria was contained only through the widespread immunization of infants and children in the last half-century. Once scientists discovered that antitoxins could be introduced into humans to fight such diseases, it was not long before pharmaceutical companies were inexpensively manufacturing these drugs on a large scale. Today, the risk of a fatal case of diphtheria is almost zero.[11]

Typhoid fever can present just as great a challenge to society: It kills a quarter of all its untreated victims. Typhoid epidemics are generally caused by contaminated water supplies, though the germ can also be spread by infected workers who handle food. That, in fact, is how Mary Mallon—better known as "Typhoid Mary"—caused the memorable outbreak of 1903. A carrier of the disease but never a victim, she worked as a food handler in New York City, and through her daily tasks managed to infect 1,300 people.

The threat of typhoid fever in this country was for the most part eliminated through technological advancements in water and sewage treatment. The use of chlorine in public water supplies was an especially effective step in preventing the spread of the bacteria *Salmonella typhi.*

Chlorine's value as a purifier was known as early as 1800, but at that time there was no system in place to protect the water supplies of large communities. Only as American cities and towns grew and prospered could they afford such an effort to protect their drinking water. Communities first developed reservoirs, then a process to treat the water before it was consumed, then a network of pipes to bring the water into people's homes, and finally additional treatment facilities to recapture the water once it had been used.

All this costs money, and only a relatively affluent society can afford it. Even today, as we approach the twenty-first century, a billion people in underdeveloped countries don't have access to clean water.[12]

There were other serious infectious diseases in America 90 years ago, ailments which, by the time I came along, seemed as remote as the horse and buggy. Pertussis, or whooping cough, a highly contagious bacterial infection, killed a higher percentage of the population in 1900 than chronic liver disease and cirrhosis do today.[13] With the development of a vaccine, the threat was reduced to insignificance by 1960. Scarlet fever has virtually been eliminated, as has polio, a crippling disease which used to strike 20,000 Americans each year.[14] Then there were yellow fever, rheumatic fever, encephalitis—the list seems endless.

My own kids, of course, will never hear about most of these deadly threats. In the nine decades between my grandmother's birth and my son's, life expectancies increased 60 percent, from 47 to 75 years, and life got a lot easier for Americans.

Drugs and chemicals were developed to combat not just the microorganisms that cause diseases, but the parasitic insects that transmit them. Our food supply became safer, with more widespread use of such things as refrigeration, packaging, preservatives, and cleaner industrial processes. In addition, our diets improved, with more access to vitamins, fresh fruits, and vegetables. Our water supply also became safer, as more and more communities modernized their sanitation facilities, along with their garbage treatment and disposal systems. Personal hygiene progressed as indoor plumbing became commonplace, making it far easier to bathe, wash clothes, and clean dishes. Additional advances in hygiene were made possible as new consumer products came on the market, like deodorant soap and household cleaners.

Wealthier and Healthier

All of these were made possible by our free-market economy. The wealthier we've grown, the healthier we've grown. In effect, capitalism, operating under a responsive system of government, has enabled us to eliminate threats that have plagued mankind from time immemorial.

Unfortunately, communicable diseases remain one of the greatest threats to people in the developing world. As a result, there is a great deal more pain and suffering, and life expectancies are often still quite low. (Life expectancy, for example, is the same today for people living in Zambia, Laos, and Bhutan as it was for Americans in 1900.)[15]

But there is hope. True, capitalism is not a magic wand. As the former Communist countries of Europe are learning, an affluent market economy takes time to develop. Still, if the lesser developed countries of the world can liberate their economies from government control and encourage private enterprise, then future generations of children there will look upon infectious diseases like typhus, cholera, and tuberculosis the way I looked upon scarlet fever—as a relic of bygone, pre-market days.

---

1. The World Bank, *World Development Report 1992—Development and the Environment* (New York: Oxford University Press, 1992), p. 5.

2. U.S. Bureau of the Census, *Historical Statistics of the United States—Colonial Times to 1970*, Part 1 (Washington, D.C., 1975), p. 55. Human life expectancy in preindustrial societies is estimated to have averaged between 30 and 33 years. See, for example, H.O. Lancaster, *Expectations of Life* (New York: Springer-Verlag, 1990), p. 8.

3. U.S. Bureau of the Census, *Historical Statistics*, p. 58.

4. U.S. Bureau of the Census, *Statistical Abstract of the United States: 1991* (Washington, D.C., 1991), p. 79.

5. U.S. Bureau of the Census, *Historical Statistics*, p. 58.

6. K. David Patterson and Gerald F. Pyle, "The Geography and Mortality of the 1918 Influenza Pandemic," *Bulletin of the History of Medicine*, 65 (Spring 1991), p. 19.

7. U.S. Bureau of the Census, *Statistical Abstract*, p. 79.

8. U.S. Bureau of the Census, *Historical Statistics*, p. 58.

9. U.S. Bureau of the Census, *Statistical Abstract*, p. 79.

10. U.S. Bureau of the Census, *Historical Statistics*, p. 58; U.S. Bureau of the Census, *Statistical Abstract*, pp. 79, 85.

11. National Center for Health Statistics, *Vital Statistics of the United States, 1988*, Vol. II, Part A (Washington, D.C., 1991), p. 93.

12. World Bank, p. 5.

13. U.S. Bureau of the Census, *Historical Statistics*, p. 58; U.S. Bureau of the Census, *Statistical Abstract*, p. 79.

14. "Infectious Diseases," *New Cyclopaedia Britannica* (1989), Vol. 21, p. 531.

15. World Bank, p. 218.

The Liberation of Women

by Bettina Bien Greaves

"Vive la différence," say the French in referring to the difference between the sexes due to physical and physiological causes. This difference can be a source of delight to those free to enjoy it, but can generate ill feeling and friction between the sexes if they are compelled by law to ignore it.[1] Our physical and physiological characteristics are bound to have economic consequences, which will persist so long as human life continues.

Legal and political rights, without distinction as to sex, have been recognized gradually by the governments of most civilized nations of the world. By legislation and common-law decisions, women have acquired freedom on a par with men to act, own property, and make contracts in their own behalf. (This freedom is being eroded by the present trend toward socialism—to the disadvantage of both men and women. Special government privileges and subsidies, progressive taxation, legislation limiting the right of contract, hours of work, and so on, have already seriously interfered with the rights of property owners and the freedom of contract. But this is another story.) For all practical purposes, laws now deal with men and women pretty much the same.

Economic Opportunities

In recent decades, economic and professional opportunities have been opened to women. Step by step, insofar as social customs have permitted, and within the limitations imposed by the "différence" between the sexes which at least the French appreciate, women in this country are relatively free. They may now compete with men, each to the extent of her abilities, in seeking their chosen goals—economically and professionally.

The tremendous advances, which have made it possible for women to achieve recognition as persons—legally, politically, economically, and professionally—are due in large part to capitalism. Savers, inven-

Mrs. Greaves, a long-time member of FEE's senior staff, is now its Resident Scholar. This article was originally published in the February 1971 issue of *The Freeman*.

tors, and producers, operating in a relatively free market economy risking their own private property in the hope of profit, supplied the goods and services that have freed women from the daily drudgery and heavy manual labor expected of them for centuries simply to fulfill their roles as sexual companions, mothers to their children, and homemakers for their families. The improved production and preparation of food, more efficient transport, better retail outlets, and inventions of modern household appliances have given women more time to pursue interests outside the home.

In this day of push-button kitchens, automatic timers, electric refrigeration, home freezers, mechanical beaters and choppers, prepared foods, and instant mixes, a housewife cannot begin to conceive of the many strenuous chores her grandmothers and great-grandmothers coped with daily. Imagine a home without heat or electricity. Imagine a kitchen without a stove, refrigerator, or running water. Suppose there were no corner stores or supermarkets with milk, butter, bread, meat, vegetables, or soap. Think of a life when each family had to grow its own food, gather the fuel to cook it, tote all water, produce the textiles, and sew, patch, and mend the family clothing.

Early Household Hints

Early cookbooks offer helpful hints to save the housewife's time and energy, hints which no modern bride need consider. For instance, keep kettles of water, both hot and cold, handy always in the kitchen. Pine wood is an economical fuel for heating ovens but hard wood makes much hotter coals. Lamps will have a less disagreeable smell if you dip your wick-yarn in strong hot vinegar, and dry it. Teach children to prepare and braid straw for their own bonnets, and their brothers' hats. Fresh meat brought into the house should be carefully covered from the flies, put in the coldest place in the cellar, and then cooked promptly—especially in summer. Save all the nice pieces of fat to make lard, and put those that are not so nice into the soap grease.

The earliest cookbooks and housekeeping manuals appeared only about 200 years ago. Few women could read before then; and how-to-do-it information, so much of which was needed to run a household smoothly, was passed along by example and by word of mouth.

Firing the Oven

One early cookbook published in this country was *The American Frugal Housewife* by Mrs. Lydia Maria Childs (12th ed., 1832). The housewife of that day cooked over an open fire, roasted meat on a spit, or baked in a reflecting oven before the fire or in a brick oven built in the chimney. To fire up the oven was such a chore that one or two days a week were set aside just for baking. With good planning, five successive bakings could be done in the oven with one heating: "The bread first—then the puddings—afterward pastry—then cake and gingerbread—and lastly, custards." This last suggestion comes from Mrs. M. H. Cornelius, whose book, *The Young Housekeeper's Friend,* appeared in 1859. At the time she wrote, brick ovens were going out, cooking stoves and ranges coming in. Yet, boiled dinners, stews, soups, and steamed cakes and puddings prepared on top of the stove were still more popular with the cooks than cakes, which called for firing up the oven.

In 1832, Mrs. Childs wrote for the rural housewife who had her own vegetable garden, a few fruit trees, and chickens. The whole family shared in the household chores, of course, and most housewives had extra help from a hired girl or a female relative living with the family. Yet, the responsibility for the work was the housewife's. She grew the herbs for flavoring, gathered the eggs, and ofttimes milked the cow. She baked with yeast of her own making, or used eggs or baking soda and cream of tartar for leavening—baking powder was not for sale until about 1850. She did the family's cooking, and did it all with crude utensils. She beat eggs with a fork or a wire whisk, and elbow grease—the rotary egg beater did not come into general use until the second half of the nineteenth century.

Housewives had to bake the family's bread regularly. This meant mixing the dough, usually in the evening, setting it to rise overnight, and kneading it "very thoroughly." Mrs. Cornelius wrote, "A half an hour is the least time to be given to kneading a baking of bread, unless you prefer, after having done this till it ceases to stick to your hands, to chop it with a chopping-knife four or five hundred strokes. An hour's kneading is not too much." Bread was the staff of life and good bread was a source of pride to the housewife.

Lack of refrigeration was a continual challenge. The housewife took care to use things before they spoiled or to find satisfactory ways to preserve them. Before the canning industry developed in the late 1800s, she had to preserve fruits and vegetables in season to be assured of provisions year-round. In 1859, Mrs. Cornelius advised putting preserves in widenecked bottles, pasting paper over the tops, and then brushing egg white over the paper with a feather to seal the bottles and discourage mold.

First, Get a Cow

The nineteenth-century housewife had to be a Jill of all trades. The Industrial Revolution with its increased specialization and division of labor barely ruffled the surface of traditional housekeeping practices. The 1859 housewife purchased a few more household items than her grandmother could have in 1832. But she still had to kill her own fowl, cut up the family's meat, salt it, smoke it, or otherwise cure it and keep it safe from bugs and animals. To be sure of good dairy products, she was told: "The first requisite is to have a good cow." Keeping a cow added to the household chores. Someone had to feed the cow and milk her, day in and day out, set the milk for the cream to rise, and churn butter at least twice a week. Without refrigeration, keeping milk, cream, butter, and dairy utensils sweet was a continual worry. Now that dairy products are sold in stores, packaged and ready to use, men do most of this heavy manual labor on a mass-production basis, using methods developed and equipment produced with the aid of increased savings and investments.

Doing the family wash was another backbreaking chore in the nineteenth century. First the soap had to be prepared from lye made out of wood ashes, and fat and grease saved from cooking. The water had to be toted and heated, heavy washtubs filled, with countless trips back and forth to the stove. After the clothes were sorted, the finest and least soiled things were washed first, the coarser and dirtier items later in the same water. Most pieces were scrubbed by hand on a washboard. The white things were boiled. After washing, rinsing, boiling, wringing, bluing, and starching as necessary, the clothes were wrung and hung outdoors on a line. Doing the family wash took another full day of the housewife's time.

Ironing consumed most of a third day each week. The flatirons and special "polishing irons" for final touchups had to be heated on the stove and reheated again and again as they cooled.

Then Came Automation

The kitchen stove or range using wood or coal gradually came into use in the mid-nineteenth century. These had advantages over the open fireplace and the brick oven. With the use of gas and the construction of gas lines in the late 1800s, new cooking jets became available—gas ovens came considerably later—making meal preparations a little easier. The development of electricity, refrigeration, large-scale specialized farming, improved transportation, professional bakeries, and the expansion of retail outlets have further liberated women from the grueling household labor which had been their lot in life. Automatic washing machines and dryers have taken the drudgery out of doing the family wash. Moth-proofed woolens and new miracle fibers have simplified the care of the family's clothing. Vacuum cleaners, floor polishers, and local dry cleaning establishments help to keep homes and their furnishings clean the year round, doing away with the need to scour the house and everything in it from top to bottom, spring and fall. Refrigeration and other effective ways of preserving foods have freed the family menu from dependence on the season. When compared with her nineteenth-century counterpart, the modern housewife is truly liberated from grinding household drudgery and endless kitchen chores.

When a housewife presses a button or turns a switch on a modern household appliance, she has at her command the labor of countless specialists—savers, investors, inventors, producers, and merchants—each of whom then helps with her daily chores. In effect, they help tote the wood when she turns up the thermostat. A twist of the faucet draws the water. Turning a dial will fire the oven. A push-button machine will wash, rinse, and wring the weekly wash. With a trip to a grocery store, the housewife can in effect grow the family's food, milk the cow, churn the butter, make the cheese, gather the eggs, knead and bake the bread, grind the spices, kill the poultry, cure the meat, preserve fruits and vegetables, and make the soap.

Capital, the Key

Each person in the world differs from every other person. Thanks to these differences, everyone benefits if each of us is free to concentrate in the field of his (or her) greatest aptitude and interest. There is some specialization and division of labor even in small groups and primitive communities. But under capitalism, with private property and the freedom to move, invest, and exchange goods and services throughout large areas and among increasingly large populations, it has been possible to develop and exploit our differences more fully than ever before, to everyone's advantage. It was this complex economic system, developed on the basis of highly specialized division of labor, which liberated women from their traditional household chores.

Women are different from men—and always will be. The modern woman has gained recognition as an individual under law. She may own property, make contracts and, thanks to the development of capitalism, now has time to pursue her special aptitudes and interests outside the home and thus compete with men economically and professionally. Rather than trying to compel denial by law of the physical and physiological differences between the sexes, let's acknowledge and accept them philosophically as the French do: "Vive la différence."

---

1. For a discussion of some effects of prohibiting discrimination on the basis of sex in economic dealings, see Gary North's "The Feminine Mistake: The Economics of Women's Liberation," *The Freeman* (January 1971), pp. 3–14.

Ferdinand de Lesseps and the Suez Canal

by George Winder

Many writers on economic history give the impression that the rugged individualists who led the economic development of the Victorian era were financial adventurers who lost the savings of the gullible with impunity, and invariably did more harm than good. Even that American classic of nineteenth-century economic history, *The Migration of British Capital* by Leland Hamilton Jenks, leaves—even if unintentionally—that impression on the mind.

Yet it was these rugged individualists who, in a few short years, laid down those railway lines upon which the world's transport still largely depends; who opened up so many of the mines of America, Africa, and Asia; and who were the chief instruments in turning primitive lands, such as Western America, Australia, South Africa, and New Zealand, into new and prosperous states.

These great leaders of enterprise who changed the face of the earth were, in the majority of cases, either British or American. But, if we are to choose one of this forgotten legion to illustrate the type at its best, then surely we must give the palm to an illustrious Frenchman, Ferdinand Marie de Lesseps.

Many great and unprecedented difficulties were overcome by the financial giants of the nineteenth century, but only the labors of Hercules can be compared with those which this intrepid venturer faced and overcame in his determination to change the geography of the world.

Before the cutting of the Suez canal, the Isthmus of Suez was a vast and empty desert. It had not changed its character since one of Napoleon's officers, François Michel de Rozière, after describing the fertility of the Nile Delta, continued: "But journey on to the Isthmus and, under the same sky, all around is changed; no trace of cultivation, no house, no shade, no greenery, no running streams, in short, nothing of use to man or beast; search the vast horizon as you may, there is nothing to arrest the eye from sea to sea but parched and lifeless desert, bare rocks, glaring sands, and utterly arid plains."

Mr. Winder, a British author, journalist, and lecturer, wrote this article for the September 1957 issue of *The Freeman*.

It was through this barren waste that de Lesseps cut a canal 100 miles in length, to join the Mediterranean and the Red Seas. Hugh Schonfield, in his books on the Suez Canal, has given us a record of de Lesseps' difficulties. The first of these was to obtain a concession that would make the work worthwhile to the investing public he hoped to interest in his project.

Egypt was normally a province of the Turkish empire, but it was governed by an Albanian adventurer, Mohammed Ali, who, after pacifying the country in the name of the Turkish Sultan, made himself viceroy and ruled with undisputed authority. He was a ruthless tyrant, but susceptible to modern ideas. He welcomed the investment of European capital in his country, and certainly became intrigued with the idea of the canal.

British Opposition

No sooner was the suggestion of a concession made to him, however, than he found himself pressed by powerful interests to leave the project alone. The most determined opponent of the canal was the British government.

Lord Palmerston, the British Prime Minister, had witnessed Napoleon's attempt to reach India by way of Egypt, and he still feared France as the greatest power in Europe. He suspected her designs in the East, and was determined that they should not be facilitated by a canal through the Isthmus of Suez. He considered that Great Britain had a perfectly good route to India around the Cape of Good Hope.

Furthermore, he looked upon the rising middle classes, with their stocks and shares and their projects for making money, with all the suspicion of the landed aristocrat. He proposed to Mohammed Ali that, instead of the canal, a railway should be built from Alexandria to Suez, which he claimed would be sufficient to deal with all the possible traffic.

Pressed by Great Britain not to build the canal, and by France and Austria not to build the railway, Mohammed Ali did nothing. In 1849 he died, and was succeeded by his grandson, Abbas. Great Britain had paid court to this young man before his succession with the result that, on attaining power, he gave his permission for the railway to be built, and the project for the canal faded into the distance. In 1854, however, Abbas was murdered by his palace slaves, and the prospects for the canal were revived. The new viceroy, Mohammed Said, was a much more civilized and intelligent ruler than his predecessor. Also, what is more to the purpose, de Lesseps, when a young man in the French consular service in Alexandria, had met him 18 years previously and made him a lasting friend.

The man destined to build the Suez Canal was living in retirement in the Manor of Chesnage, his old family home near Agnès Sorel in France, when he heard of Said's accession to power. He at once set out for Egypt.

De Lesseps was, at this time, a good-looking man in his fiftieth year, giving no other obvious sign of his great capacity than being liked by everyone he met. He possessed all the social graces, and he was a particularly good horseman—an accomplishment he would put to good use. On landing in Egypt, he was received by the viceroy with all the enthusiasm of an old friend. A villa was placed at his disposal, and he was invited to join His Highness's entourage in the forthcoming maneuvers. He was also presented with a beautiful Arab horse.

It was during these maneuvers that the great decision was made which was to have so many consequences on so many nations. Resting in the desert under the shade of a carriage, while chasseurs erected tents and built a parapet of stones around the center of an encampment, de Lesseps and Mohammed Said discussed the project of the canal. They broke off their talks during the heat of the day, but de Lesseps returned in the evening. Finding his way obstructed by the high parapet erected that morning, he put his horse at it and leaped it gracefully—a performance that is thought to have impressed favorably the viceroy's advisers, who were all cavalry officers.

Concession Granted

Be this as it may, de Lesseps certainly returned from this meeting with the coveted concession. Soon the consulates of Cairo were buzzing with unusual activity. Great Britain's opposition to the canal took the form of persuading Abdul-Mejid, the Sultan of Turkey, to exercise his rather nebulous right as the legal overlord of Egypt. De Lesseps, warned of this, hurried to Constantinople in the hope of persuading the Sultan to ratify the concession. Abdul-Mejid considered the canal plan favorably, more especially as de Lesseps pointed out that no European government was behind the undertaking. At the same time, he feared to offend Great Britain, to which country he looked for protection against the threat of Russia. In these circumstances the British ambassador at Constantinople had no difficulty in persuading him to withhold his endorsement of the concession.

De Lesseps, frustrated at the Sublime Porte, transferred his activities to the seat of the opposition—England itself. He wrote to no less a person than that very apostle of free enterprise, Richard Cobden. "How can England," he asked, "continue its incredible opposition to the Suez Canal, a private enterprise, in the origin, constitution, and object of which there is nothing to awaken any suspicion of political rivalry? How can the apostles of free trade and open competition propagate their doctrines when the two leading members of the Cabinet, who recently figured in their ranks, will not agree, through fear or horror of competition, to the suppression of a narrow neck of land which divides the two most opulent of seas, and stands as a feeble barrier against all the navies of the globe?"

He followed up this letter by visiting Great Britain. He was welcomed by shipping and mercantile interests, and addressed chambers of commerce throughout the land. Everywhere he went he obtained declarations and signatures in favor of the Canal.

He was entertained by the Royal Geographical Society, and received by Queen Victoria and the Prince Consort, who showed great interest in his project.

Skepticism Persists

It could hardly be expected, however, that one Frenchman should change the whole political outlook of Great Britain. The people who were capable of helping him were not convinced. As Justin McCarthy in his *History of Our Own Times* tells us: "Engineers showed that the canal could not be made, or at least maintained when made; capitalists proved that it never could pay; and politicians were ready to make it plain that such a canal, if made, would be a standing menace to English interests."

The Times explained to its readers that, in a land where the face of nature is changed by a tempest of wind, a single night of storm would engulf everything in the sand.

The Daily News declared: "The literature of fiction is not dead in the land of Alexandre Dumas and Monsieur de Lesseps. The most extravagant romancers are children compared with the discoverer of a new Pelusium, trying to convince his audience that 250 sick Europeans and 600 conscripted Arabs will accomplish this stupendous work, without money and without water."

The agitation in Great Britain in favor of de Lesseps was, however, strong enough to compel Palmerston to defend himself in Parliament. In doing so, he described the Canal as "an undertaking which, I believe, as regards its commercial character, may be deemed to rank among the many bubble schemes that from time to time have been palmed off on gullible capitalists. I believe that it is physically impracticable, except at expense which would be far too great to warrant the expectations of any returns. I believe, therefore, that those who embarked their money in such an undertaking would find themselves very grievously deceived by the result."

Although de Lesseps left England defeated for the time being, he nevertheless had that essential of an honest company promoter—something to sell. His famous concession was reviewed and ratified by the viceroy in 1856. This provided that the company to be formed by de Lesseps should execute the cutting of the canal at its own cost, in return for which it was to have a lease of the land necessary for its undertaking and the right to charge dues for a period of 99 years, to commence from the date of the opening of the canal.

A Great Company Is Formed

On the strength of this concession, de Lesseps decided to form his company and appeal for public subscription. Hoping to keep it free from political influence, and with the optimism typical of the company promoter, he proceeded first to allocate the number of shares that the citizens of the leading commercial nations of the world should be allowed to purchase.

Further to emphasize the company's independence of any one nation, he named it the "Compagnie *Universelle* du Canal Maritime de Suez." The capital was made up of 400,000 shares of 500 francs each, the franc then being worth about five to the dollar, and these were placed on the market in November 1858. The result was one of those setbacks the company promoter must expect. The British people—to whom, in his optimism, he had allocated 80,000 shares—took none whatever. Nor did the American investor, to whom he had hopefully allocated 20,000 shares—amounts which, we may presume, corresponded in his view with the comparative financial states of the two countries at that time.

Altogether, the citizens of some 20 nations subscribed for shares, but of these the people of Norway and Sweden, then one nation, applied for precisely one share, the people of Prussia 15, Switzerland 460, Portugal 2,719, Netherlands 2,615, and Spain 4,161. The Turks took 750 and the Egyptians 998.

The whole prospect of the Canal clearly depended upon the French people, to whom de Lesseps had allocated 80,000 shares but who fortunately applied for 207,160. Under the circumstances, these were, of course, duly allotted in full. But this still left the Company with some 177,642 shares unsold. All de Lesseps' work might yet be wrecked on those fatal financial rocks which have ruined so many imaginative undertakings.

But, at this crisis, his old friend Mohammed Said came to the rescue and subscribed for the balance of the shares. By this act, Said probably did more for Egypt than any other of its rulers. Whether this purchase by Said can be described as state aid to the company, it is a little difficult to say, for Said made no invidious distinction between himself and his country. To him the dictum of Louis XIV—"L'état, c'est moi!"—was obviously sound political thinking. The shares were registered in his own name. As we shall later see, they did eventually give a government financial stake in the company, but it was not the Egyptian government that was to enjoy this advantage.

The company had now overcome its first difficulties, but it still lacked the consent of the Sublime Porte to commence its work on the canal; and, with England using its influence with the Sultan, this seemed as unobtainable as ever.

The Operation Begins

But de Lesseps and Mohammed Said now came to a bold decision. They decided to start the work without the endorsement of Egypt's shadowy overlords. On April 25, 1859, the first shovelful of sand was moved, near the spot on which Port Said—named after the viceroy—now stands.

The work had not proceeded very far, however, before the Sultan, reminded of his ancient prerogatives, bestirred himself. He sent an imperative order to Said to stop the work at once. The viceroy, not wishing to obey, but fearful of the Sultan's power, was in a quandary. Laroche, the company's chief engineer, flatly refused to call off his men. De Lesseps appealed to Napoleon III. Fortunately, the influence of the French at the Sublime Porte was, at that time, as powerful as that of the British. Caught between opposing forces of intrigue, the Sultan failed to follow up his edict to his Egyptian viceroy, and the work went on.

The digging of the Suez Canal must be considered as one of the greatest engineering feats ever completed by mankind. Twice as long as the Panama Canal, hundreds of engineers and Europeans worked on the task, together with tens of thousands of Egyptians. For part of the distance the land was covered with salt marshes, which had to be dredged. The first undertaking was to dig a small canal from the Nile to supply the workers with fresh water.

Sandstorms, dangerous to man and covering everything in their wake, delayed progress, but the work of the canal crept steadily forward. It took three years to reach Lake Timsah, the first stage of its hundred-mile course. The mingling of the waters of the Mediterranean with those of this saltwater lake, however, proved to the world that de Lesseps' great conception was no fantasy, and that the work he had set out to perform might really be accomplished.

This did not, however, make the world any more cooperative. It seemed rather to rouse the forces of fear and jealousy to further efforts to frustrate the great Frenchman. Once more a decree from the Sublime Porte arrived, this time threatening war if the work was not stopped. The Sultan gave two reasons for his action. One was that too much Egyptian land had been alienated for the company's benefit, and, secondly, that the supply of forced labor used for the excavation of the canal deprived Egypt of the services of 60,000 persons who would be better employed elsewhere.

It is painful to read that forced labor was used for this great work, but in the Turkish Empire at that time it was the only kind of labor employed for any great undertaking.

This last effort of the Sultan to prevent the building of the canal was all the more dangerous in that de Lesseps' great supporter, Mohammed Said, was now dead. His successor, Ismail, however, who was anxious to end the claims of the Sultan, and was, in consequence, to be known as Khedive instead of viceroy, was a keen supporter of the canal. Napoleon III, appealed to once again by de Lesseps, used all his influence with Turkey, and with such effect that the Sultan appointed him as an arbitrator to settle the matter.

Under his arbitration the company gave up 150,000 acres of land and the use of its Egyptian labor but was paid a compensation of £3,000,000 by Ismail. Thus the work went on, all the more advantageously, owing to this infusion of money.

The Task Is Completed

Machinery took the place of the Egyptian laborer, and the canal crept steadily forward year after year, the investors in the company patiently waiting for the day when they might see a return on their outlay. At last, in 1869—ten years after the work had commenced—the waters of the Mediterranean and the Red Sea met, and de Lesseps' great task was done. He had overcome all the difficulties that nature and the power of governments had arrayed against him.

In November 1869, the French Imperial yacht *Aigle*, with the beautiful Empress Eugenie on board, passed through the Canal from the

Mediterranean to the Red Sea, amid the acclamations of the whole world. Ismail spent a half-million pounds on the opening celebrations. Verdi wrote his great opera *Aida* for the occasion.

The nations which for so long had laughed at de Lesseps' fantasy now made him honorable amends. Queen Victoria, as though to atone for the actions of her government, bestowed on him the Grand Cross of the Order of the Star of India; and when he visited England, he was made a freeman of the City of London. A great feast was held in his honor at the Crystal Palace. De Lesseps, the greatest of all the great promoters of enterprise in the nineteenth century, who had done more for Egypt than any of her pharaohs, now enjoyed the recognition he deserved.

How Britain Acquired Shares

Some years later, in 1875, there occurred an episode in the history of the canal company that must be recorded.

In the autumn of that year, the Khedive Ismail, who held the 176,669 shares inherited from Mohammed Said, and who was one of the most extravagant of men, was being pressed by creditors. He tried to borrow on the security of the shares. Being unable to do so, he offered them for sale in Paris.

The British Prime Minister, Benjamin Disraeli, made up his mind to purchase them for the British government. Parliament was not sitting at the time, and the Treasury would not advance money for such a purpose without its consent. Disraeli knew that delay might rob him of his opportunity. In this dilemma he bethought him of his co-religionists, Messrs. N.M. Rothschild & Sons. In them he found bankers willing to finance the deal until such time as Parliament would give its approval. In this way the British government obtained its interest in the canal, the cutting of which it had done so much to oppose. The price paid by Disraeli for the Khedive's shares was £4,080,000. The American, Leland Hamilton Jenks, valued them before World War I at £40,000,000.

The company, however, retained its private character, and the British government never obtained control of its management. The company's capital is now divided into 800,000 shares, of which the British government holds 44 per cent and appoints a minority of directors. The remaining shares are in the hands of some 100,000 Frenchmen and a few citizens of other nations.

In 1882, after rebellions and riots in Egypt in which many European lives were lost, Great Britain, at the invitation of the Khedive, occupied

Egypt for a period. This did not, however, affect in any way the private status of the canal company.

In 1888, at Constantinople, the Suez Canal Convention was signed by the leading maritime nations of the world. The first provision of this convention was as follows: "The Suez Maritime Canal shall always be free, and open in times of war as in times of peace, to every vessel of commerce or of war, without distinction of flag. Consequently, the High Contracting Parties agree not in any way to interfere with the free use of the Canal, in times of war as in times of peace. The Canal never shall be subjected to the exercise of the right of blockade."

A Triumph of Private Enterprise

The opening of the Suez Canal restored the ancient significance of the Mediterranean as a highway of world commerce. By the 1950s, some 80,000,000 tons of merchandise (more than twice the figure for the Panama Canal) and some 500,000 passengers were passing through it annually. It reduces the distance between Marseilles and Bombay by 5,800 miles. The canal company, by bringing fresh water to the Isthmus, has reclaimed thousands of acres from the desert.

The efficiency of the company's service has never been questioned, and the depth and width of the canal have been increased from time to time to keep pace with the growing tonnage of the ships which use it.

In 1956 the chairman of the International Chamber of Shipping vouched for the efficiency of the company in the following words: "We wish to put on record our recognition of the far-sighted development and first-class administration which the Shipping, therefore the Trade, of the World has enjoyed through the efforts of the Suez Canal Company for the last 87 years."

This is the great property which, on November 17, 1968, subject to certain payments for equipment, would have reverted quite legally to the Egyptian government if it only had the patience and integrity to wait. Instead, on July 26, 1956, with the company's lease still having twelve years to run, Colonel Nasser, by a forcible police action, had the heads of the company's departments placed under house arrest while armed police compelled the Egyptian banks to hand over the company's deposits. For the time being, its employees were forced to work under martial law.

In this manner the Suez Canal, that classic achievement of the age of free enterprise, became the prize of a State which did not even exist when the canal was cut. A few months later, after an abortive attempt to recover this stolen property, the statue of Ferdinand de Lesseps, which dominated the marine entrance of Port Said, was hurled from its pedestal into the sea by an Egyptian mob.

Lessons in Liberty: Hong Kong, "Crown Jewel" of Capitalism

by Robert A. Peterson

For over 100 years, the name Hong Kong has been synonymous with free enterprise. Today, the label "Made in Hong Kong" can be found just about anywhere, from clothing stores in Manhattan to gift shops in London, as the raw materials of the world are turned into finished products in Hong Kong's busy shops. To millions of tourists, Hong Kong beckons as one of the world's most alluring bargain counters. Here Swiss watches—at less-than-Swiss prices—compete with duty-free Japanese cameras and stereo equipment, and silks from Thailand glow beside bolts of Italian cloth and Harris tweed. As a result, little Hong Kong enjoys one of the highest standards of living in all Asia, second only to Japan and perhaps Singapore.

In 1987, Hong Kong—with 14 times as many people per square mile as Japan—had a per capita income of $8,260. Just a few miles away, across the Sham Chun River—in Communist China—people of the same racial stock, living in the same subtropical climate on shores washed by the same South China Sea, were able to produce a per capita income of only $300. (Incredibly, even some of that paltry sum was fueled by Hong Kong's economy, which both invests in and purchases from the mainland.)

What is it that has turned what a skeptical Lord Palmerston, in the nineteenth century, called "a barren rock" into such an economic powerhouse? What is it that has made this tiny Crown Colony (now a dependency) of the British Empire into one of the "Asian dragons" feared by protectionists in the world's largest nations?

The answer, pure and simple, is free-market economics and limited government. Throughout most of its history, Hong Kong has had no tariffs or other restraints on international trade. It has had virtually no government direction of economic activity, no minimum-wage laws, no fixing of prices, and no capital gains taxes. Despite some government intervention—in building public housing for refugees from Communist China—the British officials who govern Hong Kong have confined

---

Mr. Peterson is headmaster of The Pilgrim Academy in Egg Harbor City, New Jersey. This article was originally published in the January 1990 issue of *The Freeman*.

their role to that of umpire. They enforce the rules of the game, but do not help one side or another gain an economic advantage. As a result of these laissez-faire policies, Hong Kong has flourished.

The story of how Hong Kong came to be the "emporium of the East" is a fascinating tale of how limited government and free markets have combined to elevate one corner of China far above all the rest. In that history also lie insights for other nations whose greater resources have remained untapped because of socialistic economic policies. Now, when the world is on the verge of losing this modern exemplar of free markets and limited government—its sovereignty is scheduled to be transferred to Communist China in 1997—it is important to understand the forces that made Hong Kong what it is today. For unless right action is taken—action consistent with its history of limited government and free enterprise—Hong Kong's free-wheeling, highly creative society will be no more.

Throughout most of Chinese history, the island of Hong Kong and the nearby shore was the site of several small fishing villages that maintained a livelihood by fishing and cultivating the scanty soil. Hong Kong's greatest asset—in fact, its only natural asset—was its magnificent, almost landlocked harbor, which served as a haven from the dreaded tai-phoos ("big wind"—the origin of the English word typhoon) of the South China Sea. For many years, it was used almost exclusively by pirates. (The name Hong Kong, in Cantonese, means "fragrant harbor.") Thus, for nearly 2,000 years, the only substantial form of wealth in Hong Kong was that stolen and brought there by pirates.

The British in Hong Kong

When the British discovered Hong Kong in the 1800s—her merchant-explorers seeking to obtain Chinese tea—they immediately recognized its value and set up trading posts there to be near Canton. Unfortunately, friction soon developed between the British and Chinese, resulting in the Opium War of 1839–1842. Negotiations to prevent the war were hindered by the fact that all Europeans were considered barbarians by Chinese officials, with whom direct communication was forbidden, and by the continued smuggling of opium into China by British merchants. As a result of the Treaty of Nanking, which ended the fighting, Britain received Hong Kong Island "in perpetuity" so that her merchants might have "a port whereat they may careen and refit their ships."[1] (A subsequent treaty in 1860 gave Kowloon Peninsula to Britain while in 1898 China leased the New Territories to Britain for 99 years.)

News of the end of "hostilities" (war was never declared) was greeted with much satisfaction in England, where the ideas of free trade and nonintervention were gaining popularity. There was less rejoicing, however, at the news that the British negotiator, Sir Henry Pottinger, had exceeded his instructions and obtained Hong Kong. (The British government said it would have been satisfied with a treaty guaranteeing the security of its merchants.) Ironically, the ascendancy of the disciples of Adam Smith in England made the government hesitant to assume any more colonial responsibilities.

Yet it was precisely because free-trade ideas were on the rise that Hong Kong, from the very beginning, was set on its course as a model of free enterprise: Hong Kong would be accepted into the Empire not as a "Gibraltar of the East," as some military strategists wanted, but as an emporium of trade between East and West—a free port. The free traders viewed the British Empire not as a military empire held together by the force of arms, but as a commercial empire held together by millions of mutually beneficial relationships. These were the kinds of libertarian attitudes that helped make the period from 1815 to 1914 one of the most peaceful centuries in the history of the world.

In the early years, Hong Kong was viewed as little more than an arid rock. Lord Palmerston, the foreign minister, called it "a barren rock with nary a house upon it," while Prince Albert is supposed to have laughed when he heard that the mighty British Empire had obtained little Hong Kong. And when provoked to strong language, fashionable London ladies cried, "Go to Hong Kong!"[2]

In defense of his actions, Pottinger wrote: "the retention of Hong Kong is the only single point in which I intentionally exceeded my modified instructions, but every single hour I have passed in this superb country [China] has convinced me of the necessity and desirability of our possessing such a settlement as an emporium for our trade and a place from which Her Majesty's subjects in China may be alike protected and controlled."[3]

Hong Kong probably would have remained undeveloped, and Sir Henry would have been discredited, had it not been for its status as a free port, where virtually no duties or tariffs would be collected. Not having tariffs would provide several key advantages that would guarantee prosperity.

First, inefficient industries would be quickly eliminated, since Hong Kong entrepreneurs would be able to respond to the true vicissitudes of the market; no buggy-whip factory would outlive its usefulness shielded by a "protective" tariff.

Second, the market would direct the people of Hong Kong to do what they do best. For example, although Hong Kong has one of the world's best harbors, it has little farmland. No matter how high Hong Kong might place tariffs on foodstuffs to "protect" and encourage its own farms, it would never be able to become self-sufficient in agriculture (even though today its capitalist farmers harvest eight crops per year). Instead, Hong Kong would do better importing food—at the lowest cost possible—and servicing ships in its excellent harbor to pay for it. This is indeed what happened.

Third, free trade would allow the people of Hong Kong to buy commodities and raw materials as cheaply as possible. The money saved by not paying a tariff, duty, or tax could be used to buy additional products and materials and thus realize a higher standard of living than otherwise would be possible. Instead of sending the fruits of their labor to Great Britain in the form of customs duties, Hong Kong consumers and businessmen would be able to spend and invest this "saved" money as they saw fit. French economist Frederic Bastiat went so far as to refer to such "savings" as a gift: "When a product—coal, iron, wheat, or textiles—comes to us from abroad, and when we can acquire it for less labor than if we produced it ourselves, the difference is a gratuitous gift that is conferred upon us."[4] Hong Kong, with few natural resources, would depend on tariff-free "gifts" for its livelihood.

Finally, since resources could be obtained more cheaply, production could be enhanced, thus satisfying consumers, further improving quality and lowering costs, and creating more jobs.

An Oasis of Freedom

From the very outset, the British sought to remain true to their intention of setting up Hong Kong as an oasis of freedom—and not just for businessmen. Captain Charles Eliot, the military governor of Hong Kong, issued a proclamation that guaranteed protection for all the people and assured them that they were "further secured in the free exercise of their religious rights, ceremonies, and social customs. . . ."[5] The colony was charged with operating a limited and frugal government: the principle was stated that the British government "expects that the local revenue will be adequate to defray . . . all the . . . expenses of the government of Hong Kong," and that there should be "a strict observance of an enlightened frugality in every branch . . . of the local government."

Having no tariff income, Hong Kong's government was financed by the sale or lease of land. As far as the opium trade was concerned, the British government set forth the following policy: "The British opium smuggler must receive no protection or support, and all officials must hold aloof from so discreditable a traffic." The first ordinance passed in Hong Kong forbade all forms of slavery. This made conditions in Hong Kong consistent with the rest of the Empire, which had abolished slavery throughout its realms in the early 1800s.

Soon Victorian voluntarism began to meet the needs of the people of Hong Kong. Churches and places of worship were among the first buildings to be constructed. The London Missionary Society, under the leadership of Dr. James Legge, built the Union Chapel in 1845. American Protestant missionaries were particularly active. The first church was built by the American Baptists, followed soon after by the Catholic Church of the Immaculate Conception. The Moslems erected a mosque, while the Chinese began building their own temples. In 1849, the Anglican Church was completed, and an Anglican bishopric was established completely through private endowment. Societies of all kinds were set up. A Chinese branch of the Royal Asiatic Society, an amateur dramatic club, St. Paul's College, the Hong Kong Chamber of Commerce, and private schools for both Chinese and British were created by voluntary effort.

Although Hong Kong was a place for individualism, the flip side of individualism is not a wanton disregard for the needs of others, but the principle of voluntarism. Such voluntary and philanthropic efforts were consistent with the policies of English free traders, who thought that each colony should be able to fend for itself and create its own services.

Those who decry Western values—including the classical liberal political and economic tradition that developed in the West—should take note of the British treatment of the thousands of Chinese who flocked to live under the British flag. Tossed to and fro by the whims of despotic mandarins, quarreling war lords, and the corrupt Manchu Dynasty, the Chinese found both opportunity and near equality with the British in Hong Kong. The appointment of Chinese to responsible positions was agreed to as early as 1855. In 1857, Chinese were allowed to qualify as lawyers. In 1858, Chinese were permitted to serve as jurymen, allowed to register their ships under the British flag (if they held land in Hong Kong), and wills drawn up in accordance with Chinese usage were considered valid in court. The British also extended equal treatment to the boat people, or Tanka. For centuries, Chinese law forbade them to settle ashore, marry landowners, or take government examinations. Such discrimination ended under British rule and the Chinese population grew from 20,338 in 1848 to 121,825 in 1865.

Despite all the advantages the British gave to the Chinese, it was no one-way street. In 1894, Lord Ripon wrote to Governor Sir William Robinson: "under the protection of the British Government, Hong Kong has become a Chinese rather than a British community . . . and Chinese settlement . . . has been one main element in its prosperity."[6]

Throughout the nineteenth century, Hong Kong's business pursuits were centered around shipping and trade. In 1881, over 3,200 ships entered Hong Kong. That same year over 24,000 Chinese junks also passed through the harbor. To service these ships, there were 400 ship chandler shops, 20 rope factories, 93 boat works, two cannon foundries, and one dry dock. To handle all the transactions that went along with these services, many banks were founded or established in Hong Kong, including the Oriental Bank; the Mercantile Bank of India, Australia, and China; the Hong Kong and Shanghai Bank; and the United Service Bank.[7]

Into the Twentieth Century

In the twentieth century, a new phase of Hong Kong history began: over the next 80 years Hong Kong would become a refuge for millions of Chinese fleeing persecution, instability, and violence, a home to millions of people, an industrial dynamo, as well as the site of a great airport built on land reclaimed from the sea.

The influx of refugees came in six major waves in the twentieth century. The first wave came in 1911, as a result of the revolutions that overthrew the Manchu Dynasty and established the Republic of China. The second wave came in 1937, after Japan invaded China. During World War II, Hong Kong was captured by Japan. Cut off from world markets, the island languished. More than one million Chinese left Hong Kong and returned to mainland China. Since both were ruled by the heavy hand of Japanese militarism, there was little advantage to staying in Hong Kong. The third wave began in 1949 when the Communists took over China.

A fourth wave of immigration occurred in 1962, when widespread starvation—the result of Communist China's socialist land-use policies—forced thousands of Chinese to emigrate. In one 25-day period in 1962, Communist Chinese border guards allowed 70,000 Chinese to walk to freedom in Hong Kong. The Cultural Revolution in the late 1960s sent another human wave into Hong Kong, while the 1970s saw over 100,000 Vietnamese boat people find refuge there. Fourteen thousand were given permanent resident status, while 100,000 were permitted to work in Hong Kong pending transfer to permanent homes abroad.[8]

In the years after World War II, Hong Kong took advantage of the human capital from Communist China, and began producing goods that appeared in markets all over the world. With few raw materials, no local sources of power such as coal and oil, and shortages of land and water, Hong Kong developed one of the fastest growing economies in the world.

From 1,050 separate industries, employing 64,000 people in 1947, the figure rose to 17,239 industries employing 589,505 in 1970. Most of the factories were still family concerns, using their own "capital"—including family members' hard work—to produce quality goods at low prices. By 1970 the textile industry employed 30 percent of the work force and produced 40 percent of total exports. Plastics accounted for 12 percent of exports; electronics, 10 percent. Highly developed countries, such as Great Britain and America, began "protecting" themselves by asking Hong Kong to impose "voluntary" quotas on many of its exports. By this time, Hong Kong's trade volume had passed that of much larger countries, such as New Zealand.[9]

In the early 1980s, realizing that socialism had failed to produce a healthy economy, the People's Republic of China established four Special Economic Zones where its people could learn the world's economic ways. All the zones were set up in southeast China, and for good reason: to be near Hong Kong. Since that time, investment capital, visitors, and Hong Kong know-how have crossed the border to quicken the pace of Chinese economic development. Shenzhen, the largest and most successful of the economic zones, is located directly across the border. In 1983, of some 1,600 government-approved contracts, about 50 percent were with Hong Kong firms. Short of space, Hong Kong entrepreneurs were using land in China for everything from country clubs to cemeteries.[10]

Today, little Hong Kong—which fuels its own vibrant economy as well as much of China's—has more than 150 banks, four stock exchanges, and is the world's third largest financial center. It is the third largest diamond and gold trading center, the largest manufacturer of toys, and the second largest maker of watches. It has an infant mortality rate lower than that of either Britain or the United States, and one of the highest protein-consumption rates in the world. In the early 1980s, during a worldwide recession, Hong Kong had a maximum 5.2 percent unemployment rate when Britain's was more than twice as high. Over two million tourists visit annually, to shop in this oasis of freedom where East meets West. Chinese author Han Su Yin described Hong Kong as "the deep roaring bustling eternal market . . . where life and love and souls and blood and all things made and grown under the sun are bought and sold and smuggled and squandered."[11] Fueled by free trade, Hong Kong's growth rate from 1975 to 1987 was 11.8 percent, while Communist China's was only 4.3 percent.

A recent Fodor's tourist guidebook to Hong Kong and Macau has this to say about "Doing Business": "Hong Kong is one of those rare places on earth that plays the free-trade game according to the classical rule. . . . A national of any country may do business or set up business (so long as it is legal). . . . The rules of business in Hong Kong are few. Whether you are a visiting businessperson or a potential entrepreneur, you will not go far wrong if you remember this: You are in a 'free country.' If you succeed, you can take all the credit; if you fail, you must take all the blame. The authorities give some help (but no subsidies, tax reliefs, or featherbeds); what is more important, they don't hinder you. . . . There is no capital gains tax. . . . [I]ncome arisen from abroad goes tax free. . . . The Hong Kong salaries tax return is one simple sheet. . . . There is no income tax withholding. . . . The government's intervention in business affairs is minimal."[12] Milton Friedman has called Hong Kong "the modern exemplar of free markets and limited government."[13]

No Utopia

Hong Kong is no utopia: never has been, never will be. A nexus between East and West, it has always been a center of opium trade— first legal, now illegal. It is one of the most crowded places on earth, and hence, there is little tolerance for new refugees. There are great disparities between rich and poor. Yet there appears to be little discontent about the division of wealth because of the opportunity for advancement. Yesterday's shanty dweller lives in a resettlement block today; tomorrow—if he works hard—he may live in upscale Repulse Bay.

Unfortunately, Hong Kong's days are numbered. In 1984, Britain signed a Joint Declaration with Communist China, turning over sovereignty of the New Territories (over 90 percent of the colony) to China in 1997. China guaranteed that the capitalist system would last for at least 50 years and that democratic institutions would be preserved. Their slogan for the union: "one country, two systems."

Hong Kong has not reacted well to the negotiations or the settlement. From 1981 to 1983, stock-market prices fell 50 percent. The budget for 1983–84 incurred a deficit, something unheard of in Hong Kong, which believes in surpluses. Billions of dollars flowed out of Hong Kong, so much that neighbors like the Philippines, Thailand, and Malaysia set up programs to attract its panic money.

Hong Kongians had hoped that Britain would give them British citizenship or the "right of abode" on British soil if they had to flee the Communists. So far, the British haven't acted. Unlike people in "dependencies" belonging to other countries, those in British dependencies don't automatically have British citizenship. As a result, even before the massacres in Tiananmen Square, a mass exodus began. In 1986, 19,000 residents left; in 1987, 30,000; in 1988, 45,000.

The exodus is carrying away some of the city's most productive citizens—professionals and middle managers. Seventy-five percent of all pharmacists are planning to emigrate before China takes over in 1997; shortages among police, fire, and judicial officers are already growing serious. After 1984, many people began leaving Hong Kong for a time to live in countries like Canada, the United States, and Australia in order to qualify for a foreign passport. Then they can return to Hong Kong safe in the knowledge that if things go bad, they have a refuge.[14]

The massacre in Tiananmen Square and the deception that followed have only confirmed Hong Kong's fears. Polls taken immediately after the Beijing massacre indicate that most Hong Kongians don't want to leave—Hong Kong is their home. Yet to stay would place them under the same coercive government from which they and their parents fled. "The majority of people in Hong Kong feel helpless," says Jonathan Chao, director of the Chinese Church Research Center there. One prominent lawyer went so far as to say, on Hong Kong television, that "For England to give 5.5 million people to Communist China is like giving 6 million Jews to the Nazis."[15]

Supporting the idea that all Hong Kongians should be given British citizenship, Frank Ching, writing in the *Wall Street Journal*, explains:

"No other democracy denies a dependent people the right to self-determination or forces them to live under a Communist government.

"No other democracy issues passports that do not entitle their holders to enter the country that issued the passports.

"When British Gibraltar and the Falklands were threatened with takeover by another country, Britain offered the people protection by giving them full-citizenship rights.

"Hong Kong is the only exception. The British are now preparing to hand over its 5.5 million people to a Communist government. The decent thing for Britain to do is to restore the citizenship rights of the people in Hong Kong. It is the only way remaining to salvage Hong Kong and restore British honor."[16]

As Ching points out, even if the British acknowledge that the land was on a lease, the people are not. As such, they should be given full citizenship rights—much as the U.S. has extended rights to Puerto Ricans, and Holland has given full rights to her dependents in the Netherlands Antilles and Aruba. British citizenship would be something the Communist Chinese couldn't take away, if and when they dismantle Hong Kong's free-market system. It might even ensure that China wouldn't tamper with Hong Kong's market.

In the light of Tiananmen Square, the British should use every means to renegotiate the joint accords, telling the Chinese that what happened there was not acceptable. The Tiananmen Square massacre—set against the backdrop of China's historic political instability and isolationism—makes it inconceivable that Communist China would allow Hong Kong to continue its Western contacts—including Western newspapers with their stock market reports, its aviation and shipping treaties, its checkbook accounts (which are not permitted in Communist China) and myriads of other capitalistic institutions.

China's Communist regime is trapped in a catch-22 situation: the only thing that can save its economy—a free market such as exists in Hong Kong—is the very thing that will reduce the regime's totalitarian powers by giving power to entrepreneurs and consumers. So far, whenever Communist leaders have had to choose between a better economy or keeping power concentrated in their hands, they have always chosen the latter. To allow Hong Kong to continue "business as usual" after 1997 would guarantee a heavy flow of ideas on liberty, and that, as the world saw in the summer of 1989, the present Chinese government cannot tolerate. It was apparently Deng Xiaoping who ordered the army to fire on the students, the same man who signed the Hong Kong accord with Margaret Thatcher.

Ironically, Communist China would be the chief beneficiary of continued British sovereignty over Hong Kong. Hong Kong accounts for at least 35 percent of China's annual foreign exchange earnings. China also benefits from Hong Kong's financial services, port facilities, and skills in marketing Chinese products. All this will most likely change when Hong Kong passes into Chinese hands. China threatens to kill the goose that lays the golden egg.

---

1. G.B. Endacott, *A History of Hong Kong*, 2nd ed. (Hong Kong: Oxford University Press, 1964, 1988), p. 22.

2. John Scofield, "Hong Kong Has Many Faces," *National Geographic* (January 1962), p. 4.

3. Endacott, *National Geographic* (January 1962), p. 22.

4. George C. Roche III, *Frederic Bastiat: A Man Alone* (New Rochelle, N.Y.: Arlington House, 1971), p. 53.

5. Endacott, p. 26.

6. Endacott, p. 215.

7. Endacott, p. 195.

8. *Fodor's Hong Kong and Macau* (New York: Fodor's Travel Guides, 1987), p. 25.

9. Harry Robinson, *Monsoon Asia: A Geographical Survey* (New York: Praeger, 1967), p. 476.

10. John J. Putnam, "China's Opening Door," *National Geographic* (July 1983), pp. 64–83.

11. *Fodor's Hong Kong and Macau*, p. 58.

12. Fodor, pp. 106–109.

13. Milton and Rose Friedman, *Free to Choose* (New York: Harcourt Brace Jovanovich, 1980), p. 34.

14. Frank Ching, "Hong Kong's Hopes Wane as Britannia Waives the Rules," *Wall Street Journal*, April 19, 1989, p. A19.

15. These impressions were gained from telephone interviews with an American student in Hong Kong through the month of June 1989; Jonathan Chao, quoted in *World*, July 1, 1989, p. 7.

16. Ching, p. A19.

III. THE CASE FOR FREE TRADE

Free Trade, Freedom of Enterprise, and All That

by Donald B. Billings and Ellis W. Lamborn

The current low price [1977] for the world's "surplus" sugar has in recent weeks brought to center stage a conflict which is always lurking just beneath the surface of conversation, namely the extent to which Americans really do or do not believe in the "free market philosophy." Our attempted defense of free trade and the free enterprise system has elicited heated criticism from a community nominally devoted to the "free market" order. The chairman of a major sugar company is disappointed in our decision "to champion a 'free market' philosophy, as is popular in academic circles." The president of an association of beet growers suggests that he is "a firm believer in the free market and free trade [but] free trade in sugar is a horse of a different color." It would seem that the commitment to a free-market system of economic institutions is only for the other guy. Our own horse is always of a different color.

Fortunately the appeal and defense of free markets in which new producers, foreign and domestic, are free to enter and compete does not exist "only in texts." The drafters of our Constitution saw the great wisdom of prohibiting restrictions on the flow of goods and services across state lines by explicitly providing in Article 1, Section 10, that "No State shall, without the Consent of Congress, lay any Imposts or Duties on Imports or Exports, except what may be absolutely necessary for executing its inspection Laws." The European Economic Community (Common Market) has copied this phenomenally successful U.S. experiment in free trade in the Treaty of Rome, creating a customs union in which goods and services flow freely across national boundaries. These experiments in economic unification for the purpose of increasing the extent of the market and the degree of economic specialization have been extraordinarily successful in raising wages, salaries and incomes.

Those who argue that a particular industry should be subsidized and protected from foreign competition in order to provide for "orderly" and "stable" markets would, presumably, also be in favor of

This article was originally published in the February 1977 issue of *The Freeman*. At the time, Professors Billings and Lamborn taught in the Department of Economics at Boise State University in Idaho.

amending the U.S. Constitution so that Idaho might place quotas on the "surplus" automobiles imported from Michigan, the "surplus" oranges from Florida, or the "surplus" farm machinery from Ohio. Likewise, we should be up in arms over the subsidies that the state of Pennsylvania has recently negotiated for the assembly of Volkswagen Rabbits in the U.S., on the grounds that the subsidies will provide an unfair advantage for the Pennsylvanians. Shouldn't we be angry that Pennsylvania has seen fit to have their taxpayers subsidize our automobile purchases?

On the other hand, Idaho would presumably not be too appreciative of a decision by California (fortunately precluded by the U.S. Constitution) to place a quota on "surplus" Idaho potatoes. We can't have it both ways. Free trade and economic specialization increase real incomes or it does not! We believe in the "free enterprise" system (with all of its weaknesses and uncertainties for individual economic values which need to be dealt with in an enlightened manner) or we don't.

Low Foreign Wages

The traditional low-foreign-wages argument once again emerges as an argument for protection. It is argued that one of the reasons for the lower dollar cost of many foreign goods is the high "level of wages paid in the United States, including the domestic sugar industry, compared to those paid in foreign countries." Unfortunately, the argument is unsound. Relatively high wages are a result of high productivity, and relatively low wages are a result of low productivity. If American labor has high wages, it is because American labor has higher man-hour productivity than foreign labor.

If low foreign wages are the source of our troubles, then why is it the case that U.S. wages are highest in the very industries in which we are *most* competitive? Why do we dominate world markets for commercial airframes, computers, construction machinery, mineral mining machinery, communications equipment, medical instruments, and the like? These are industries with high skill and engineering labor requirements in which wages and salaries dwarf those in the sugar beet growing and processing industries. Comparative advantage and specialization are predicated on economic efficiency and *not* technical or engineering efficiency. Yield per acre is totally irrelevant. What matters are the relative prices and endowments of the different human and nonhuman productive agents used in the production process.

If labor is "cheap" abroad, we should be cultivating its use in those industries which use relatively more unskilled and semiskilled labor, and be making efforts simultaneously to transfer our more productive (i.e., high wage) labor force into those industries in which a productivity advantage, arising from technology, marketing, skill levels, and the like, is demonstrated. The Trade Reform Act of 1974 provides for liberal doses of "adjustment assistance" to ease the movement of labor and capital to the relatively more productive sectors of the American economy.

If the United States can export its environmentally destructive industries to more hospitable (clean) areas of the world which have a greater remaining capacity to absorb pollutants, then let it be done. To argue that a domestic industry is deserving of protection because it is forced to absorb the full social costs of environmentally destructive productive processes, not only argues for inefficiency but also ignores a fundamental truth. If the rest of the world is willing to give us sugar, rubber products, textiles, beef, automobiles, stereo components at a lower real resource cost than they can be made available from domestic resources, then it is to our advantage—providing we are interested in higher real incomes for the American people—to let them "dump" their productive resources in the United States.

It Takes Two to Trade

Of course, this is a two-way street. When trade has developed between nations, restrictions on exports will reduce that nation's capacity to import foreign products, the result being lower living standards in both the exporting and importing countries. The embargoes on our exports of wheat and soybeans in recent years are examples of this wrong-headed policy.

The fundamental error of logic of those who want "free markets" for the other guy and "orderly" markets for themselves was well exposed in 1846 by Frederic Bastiat in his imaginary petition to the French Chamber of Deputies. His satirization of the protectionist fallacy was in the name of free trade and freedom of enterprise. He entitled it a "Petition from the Manufacturers of Candles, Waxlights, Lamps, Chandeliers, Reflectors, Snuffers, Extinguishers; and from Producers of Tallow, Oil, Resin, Alcohol, and in General Everything That Concerns Lighting."

> Gentlemen, you are right: you reject abstract theories. As practical men, you are anxious only to free the producer from foreign competition and secure the *national market* to *national labor.*

We now offer you an admirable opportunity to apply your practice. We are subjected to the intolerable competition of a foreign rival whose superior facilities for producing light enable him to flood the French market at so low a price as to take away all our customers the moment he appears, suddenly reducing an important branch of French industry to stagnation. This rival is the sun.

We request a law to shut up all windows, dormers, sky-lights, openings, holes, chinks, and fissures through which sunlight penetrates. Our industry provides such valuable man-ufactures that our country cannot, without ingratitude, leave us now to struggle unprotected through so unequal a contest.

Do not repulse our petition as a satire without hearing our reasons. Your protection of artificial lighting will benefit every industry in France. If you give us the monopoly of furnishing light, we will buy large supplies of tallow, coal, oil, resin, wax, alcohol, silver, iron, bronze, and crystal. Greater tallow con-sumption will stimulate cattle and sheep raising. Meat, wool, leather, and above all manure, that basis of agricultural riches, will become more abundant. Greater oil consumption will stimulate cultivation of the luxuriant olive tree. Resinous trees will cover our heaths. Swarms of bees will gather upon our mountains the perfumed treasures now cast useless upon the winds. In short, granting our petition will greatly develop every branch of agriculture.

Navigation will equally profit. Thousands of vessels will soon be employed in whaling, and thence will arise a navy capable of upholding the honor of France. [Note the defense argument.]

Paris will become magnificent with the glittering splendor of gildings, bronzes, crystal chandeliers, lamps, reflectors, and candelabras. When we and our many suppliers have become rich, our great consumption will contribute to the prosperity of workers in every industry. No one, not even the poor resin manufacturer amidst his pine forest nor the miserable miner in his dark dwelling, will fail to enjoy an increase of salary and comforts. There is perhaps not one Frenchman, from the rich stockholder to the poorest match-seller, who is not interested in the success of our petition.

We foresee your objections, gentlemen; but there is not one which you will not have to take from the free-traders and which is not opposed to your practice. Do you object that the consumer must pay the price of protecting us? You have yourselves already answered the objection. When told that the consumer is interested in free importation of iron, coal, corn, wheat, cloth, etc., you have answered that the producer is interested in their exclusion. You have always acted to *encourage labor, to increase the demand for labor.*

Will you say that sunlight is a free gift, and that to repulse free gifts is to repulse riches under pretense of encouraging the means of obtaining them? Take care—you deal a death-blow to your own policy. Remember: hitherto you have always repulsed foreign produce because it was an approach to a free gift; and the closer this approach, the more you have repulsed the goods. You have, in obeying the wishes of other monopolists, acted only from a *half-motive;* to grant our petition there is a much *fuller inducement.* To turn us down just because our case is much stronger than any previous one would be to accumulate absurdity upon absurdity.

When we buy a Portuguese orange at half the price of a French orange, we in effect get it half as a gift. If you protect national labor against the competition of a *half-gift,* what principle justifies allowing the importation of something just because it is *entirely a gift*? You are no logicians if, refusing the half-gift as hurtful to human labor, you do not with double zeal reject the full gift.

The difference in price between an imported article and the corresponding French articles is a *free gift* to us. The bigger the difference, the bigger the gift. It is as complete as possible when the producer gives us his goods entirely free, as the sun does with light. The question is whether you wish for France the benefit of free consumption or the supposed advantages of laborious production. Choose, but be consistent. And is it not the height of inconsistency to check as you do the importation of foreign goods merely because and even in proportion as their price approaches zero, while at the same time you freely admit the light of the sun, whose price during the whole day is at *zero*?

Free Trade and Prosperity: A Global Approach

by Steven E. Daskal

Americans are especially prone to feel obligated to help others on a global scale. Whether it is the unfortunate plight of our fellows in the underdeveloped nations, often known as the "Third World," or the difficulties and unemployment facing some Americans at home, we care. Within that context, free trade is a vital issue, because it is one of the primary means by which the market economy helps create global prosperity.

When surveying the world economic situation, some Americans feel guilt over our comparative wealth and comfort in contrast to the millions living at the subsistence level. Our size, power, and wealth appear to some as being of little value unless we use that wealth to help the less fortunate. We send food, money, training advisors, educators, and missionaries around the world in a sincere effort to help others. These efforts have been undertaken by individuals, religious and social organizations, charitable associations, and the government. As believers in voluntarism and limited government, it is inappropriate for us to criticize how individuals freely spend their money. However, when the government coerces us through taxation to send aid overseas, we often have cause to object to the way our involuntary contribution is being spent on activities that appear unnecessary, wasteful, or even counterproductive.

Sometimes efforts to feed the starving prove well-intentioned, but sadly ineffectual. Even if the entire U.S. budget were directly distributed to the poorer half of the world's population, it would amount to less than $1,000 per person, certainly not enough to cure global poverty. Of course, with both our own bureaucracy and that of the recipient nation serving as intermediaries, a lot of that $1,000 would never reach the poor, but would instead support a small army of administrators, investigators, analysts, and auditors in both countries. If the recipient country's government were less than scrupulously honest, as is all too often the case, the poor would wind up with a couple of cups of milk and grain, while the U.S. government would be bankrupt. After

---

Mr. Daskal, a defense systems analyst and writer, resides in Springfield, Virginia. This article was originally published in the February 1986 issue of *The Freeman*.

decades of receiving such aid, the recipient country would still be poor, and in fact there would be more poor people to feed in the future. One would hope that a better way to help these people would have been discovered by now.

Maximizing Employment

While we continue to be concerned about the poor overseas, we also feel an obligation to ensure maximum employment of our own citizens. Unemployment is generally recognized as a significant problem, for both personal and social reasons. Given current law, the financial drain the unemployed place upon society through the wide range of "compensation" and support programs is also of growing concern. While in most cases, the value of the welfare benefits an individual can receive is less than working wages, welfare pays well enough to support many people for extended periods of time. As government regulations and compensation plans directly and indirectly increase the cost of labor, and commensurately decrease the average worker's net pay, more and more businesses find it less profitable and more difficult to hire workers. Thus, unemployment, like global poverty, seems unlikely to disappear, despite the growing expenditures attempting to combat it. The more the government spends and regulates, the fewer people can be hired by private enterprise.

A popular scapegoat for unemployment in the United States (and in many other "industrialized" nations) is the "trade deficit." Many people, especially manufacturers and unionized workers, see imported vehicles, electronics, machine tools, and textiles flooding our markets and "taking away" sales from American manufacturers. These lost sales translate, they contend, into reduced production requirements, and ultimately lost American jobs. The fact that imported goods create sales, financing, service, and other related employment is generally ignored because domestic industrial workers and manufacturers are far better organized, have more political clout, and are much more vocal. The result is a periodic frenzy of proposals to "protect American jobs and industry" through tariffs and quotas intended to limit or eliminate imports. As natural and unavoidable consequences of such moves:

- the cost of a given item to the American consumer rises due to the higher cost of producing the American product and the loss of competitive pressure on prices;
- consumers have less choice and fewer products available for purchase, reducing the incentive to increase earnings;

- the overall strength of the American economy falters as consumer spending drops in response to rising prices;
- Americans involved in buying and selling imported goods
  would be faced with significant losses and possibly unemployment;
- manufacturers lose business, resulting in higher unemployment,
  lower tax revenues, and higher government spending in foreign
  countries;
- foreign individuals, corporations, and governments have fewer
  dollars to buy U.S. goods and services, or to pay off their heavy
  debt burdens; and
- growing economic problems in foreign nations often lead to
  political instability and increased anti-Americanism, increasing
  requirements for non-productive defense spending both overseas and in the United States.

Protectionism, like any other form of government intervention in
economic life, has a cost. Government tariffs and quotas transfer money
to certain people who have invested in, manage, or work for, industries
that aren't competitive on their own merits. This forced transfer guar-
antees these firms that they will have a greater market share than they
would have had without protection from competition. Without facing
the pressures of the free market, they can continue to produce more
expensive, less desirable goods, knowing their market cannot be taken
by foreign competitors. Thus, the consumers (which often include the
people benefiting from the protection) pay for protection—they get
less, and pay more.

Protectionism Costs Consumers Billions

How much do we pay, as consumers, for protection of a few industries? Michael Munger, in "The Costs of Protectionism," estimates the
total burden (in 1980 dollars) to be over $58 billion, and it is probably
even greater today. Nearly a third of that cost was in the textile and
apparel market, a burden that fell most heavily on the poor, who tend
to buy the least expensive clothing that doesn't look cheap. They
tended to favor foreign-made goods because they looked good, and
didn't cost as much as American-made items. This value differential
existed despite the tariffs and quotas involved, but it was greatly
reduced. While the more affluent could afford the higher prices or even
switch to American products, the poor were faced with buying less.

Six billion dollars worth of tariffs and other barriers were applied to agricultural products, another area where the poor pay the cost for protectionism. On the other hand, protecting the jobs of highly paid auto, steel, and machinery production workers (and their employers) accounted for $26 billion in added protection costs. These costs affect all of us in a myriad of ways, because higher-priced transportation and manufacturing equipment raises the cost of all commodities to the consumer. Since these indirect costs are not included in the $26 billion, the true cost of protectionism in this segment of the economy could in fact be far higher.

Despite the "chance to modernize and catch up" that protection was supposed to offer these industries, most of them have chronically cried for protection against imports for decades. Only the threat of protection being phased out forced automakers and some steel manufacturers to begin modernizing. Some still haven't, and are slowly crumbling despite protection. The loss of employment in various aspects of importing and exporting goods is another unknown cost.

Another common cause of pleas for protection is the accusation that foreign states are selling goods in the U.S. at a price lower than it costs the foreign manufacturer to produce them. This practice, known as "dumping," is more often a reflection of some economist's incorrect analysis of the cost of production of a given item, rather than an example of some competing nation's attempts to undermine our economy. True "dumping" results in the "dumper" losing money on every piece sold, while the recipient, an American consumer, has saved money that can be invested elsewhere. True "dumping" will ultimately bankrupt the "dumper."

The French economist and legislator Frederic Bastiat recognized the fallacy of protectionism in the 1840s. He often resorted to satire to illustrate the absurdity of being preoccupied with maintaining a "favorable balance of trade." One of these was so believable that many thought it was a good example of the benefits of protection!

> A French merchant shipped $50,000 worth of goods to New Orleans and sold them for a profit of $17,000. He invested the entire $67,000 in American cotton and shipped it back to France. Thus, the customhouse record showed that the French nation had imported more than it had exported—an *unfavorable* balance of trade. Very bad.
>
> At a later date, the merchant decided to repeat the personally profitable transaction. But just outside the harbor his ship was sunk in a storm. Thus, the customhouse record showed that the French nation had exported more products than it had

imported—a *favorable* balance of trade. Very good. Additionally, more jobs were thereby created for shipbuilders.

Since storms at sea are undependable, perhaps the safest government policy would be to record the exports at the customhouse and then throw the goods into the ocean. In that way, the nation could guarantee to itself the profit that results from a favorable balance of trade.

That economic disaster results from trade restriction and protectionism is not just theoretical speculation, however. The events of the period between 1922 and World War II illustrate them very graphically. The mid-1920s was a period of generally increasing prosperity. However, then as now, the rapid changes in economic organization, management and technology had severe impact on a few outdated industries that relied heavily on manual labor, and hurt those farmers who were still using nineteenth-century techniques.

Jude Wanniski, a former member of the *Wall Street Journal*'s editorial staff, wrote a book entitled *The Way the World Works*. He describes the manner in which the beleaguered "low-tech" manufacturers and farm lobbyists pushed through the infamous Smoot-Hawley Tariff act. The idea of keeping out foreign competition sounded good to the news media, but it terrified the bankers and investors of Wall Street. When it appeared certain the bill would be passed, the stock market panicked. The result was the stock market crash of the autumn of 1929, followed by the Depression that was fueled by the general collapse of world trade. Consumers in America and the rest of the world were forced to buy inefficiently produced domestic goods, or pay extortionate prices for foreign ones. Foreign governments of course retaliated in kind, many having already begun economic warfare against the rest of the world. Markets for American goods dried up, investment collapsed, businesses failed, jobs disappeared.

Despite the popular belief that laws passed since 1929 could prevent another Great Depression, it *could* happen again. America is far more dependent upon imports and exports today than it was in the 1920s. A global trade war would have disastrous consequences at home, and could create enormous security problems for us abroad. As reliant as we are upon free trade, the rest of the world is even more dependent upon it, even though they may not recognize it. A collapse of world trade would hurt virtually all of our allies, and threaten the survival of many developing nations barely able to avoid default on their debts.

If one looks at things from a sufficiently broad perspective, one begins to see a major contradiction in our foreign policy. On the one hand, we want to help the poor overseas, and try to do so at great expense, but with limited success. We spend great sums of money to help defend foreign nations from present and potential enemies. Yet, on the other hand, we are willing to threaten the economic and political stability of these same nations (and our own) by creating insurmountable walls against their ability to freely sell goods in the world's richest market—the United States. This is a significant and costly inconsistency.

We have sent aid money to strengthen the economies of countries such as Japan, Thailand, Israel, Italy, Turkey, South Korea, and Germany (to name a few). If these nations are to develop strong economies, they will naturally try to export goods to the United States and other nations. Yet, our response is to consider tariffs to shut out their products—threatening the same economies we ostensibly wanted to develop. The consumer ultimately pays the bill for all of this. They pay taxes to support efforts aimed at creating productive enterprises overseas, and pay higher prices (and have less free choice) because of attempts to protect American businesses against competition from overseas. And, as the ultimate blow to the budget and good sense, we pay to defend the same nations that supposedly "threaten" American jobs and profits.

The Benefits of Free Trade

Americans sincerely want to help people overseas. The question has become *how* to help them to the greatest extent while spending the least of our own hard-earned money. We also care about the health of our economy. Once again, the question is *how* to help preserve U.S. economic prosperity without disrupting international trade and causing ever-higher prices. The best method for accomplishing both goals is through free trade!

Why free trade? A basic economic reality—buying the best goods at the lowest prices—makes free trade more economical than closing our markets to foreign competitors. American consumers (all of us, including businesses and unionized labor) benefit by obtaining more goods for less money, while the foreign manufacturers and workers benefit by having jobs, making profits, and paying taxes to governments which then have a better chance to pay off their enormous debts. This, in turn, will make American banks more secure.

Free trade allows consumers around the world to buy more for less, which in turn creates more revenue for businesses. Governments have less call to provide tax-supported benefits to individuals or businesses, thus relieving the need to continue increasing taxes, inflation, or deficits. Ultimately, free trade will allow all but the poorest, least educated, and least diligent nations to get ahead. Examples of this are easy to find.

The most successful of the developing countries, states such as Singapore, the Republic of Korea, Republic of China (Taiwan), and Hong Kong, have built themselves up from illiteracy and poverty largely due to their respect for the power of free trade and relative economic freedom. Potentially wealthy developing nations, such as China, Brazil, Argentina, Nigeria, and Mexico, have stifled their own economic development through confused myriads of protective tariffs, import quotas, and centralized government manipulation of the economy.

Free trade also helps Americans and our trading partners overseas increase national security against both invasion and subversion. Open trade tends to improve the economic health of all trading nations. These nations tend to be more stable internally, since strong economies generally result in reduced unemployment, greater availability and affordability of food, clothing, and other commodities, and relief from the sense of desperation felt by people barely able to survive—a desperation that often leads to disorder and revolution. These increasingly self-sufficient nations also are better able to defend themselves against invasion. Their industries are strong, their people are more confident, and they are able to obtain necessary imported supplies easily. Thus, nations dedicated to free trade tend to be more valuable as friends and allies, and less of a liability needing continuous costly support and military assistance.

If this sounds too easy, too good to be true, just reflect on the benefits we gained in our own country by the elimination of trade restrictions between the colonies/states after the adoption of the Constitution. Free trade allowed for better direction of local economic activity. New Englanders didn't have to struggle to be self-sufficient in agriculture on their rocky soil, while Southerners could freely purchase better, less costly tools and machinery built in large New England and mid-Atlantic factories. Entire new industries developed to support this commerce, as evidenced by the growth of banks and by the flurry of railroad, steamship, and canal companies that were formed in the nineteenth century. While inflexible individuals and businesses may have suffered, the overall prosperity of all of the states increased dramatically, and employment grew rapidly despite the destruction of the Civil War and the influx of impoverished immigrants from around the world.

Free trade works, both in the context of international development and in ensuring greater domestic prosperity. It helps the poor and at the same time helps the working class, the middle class, and the wealthy. It works because it represents efficiency—from each according to his ability, to each according to his work (work in the scientific sense of energy expended that has a tangible result). Money is not wasted administering complex trade agreements, monitoring the "fairness" of international trade practices, or buying overpriced goods. Money is not involuntarily taken from taxpayers to subsidize inefficient American businesses or the poor overseas.

Open international trading relations, especially between private individuals and businesses, facilitates peaceful relations between nations. Warfare is often a costly, destructive, and unsuccessful means to acquire another nation's goods and services—trade is a far more efficient and mutually beneficial way to obtain the desired goal. Free trade is a sound basis for relations between free nations. It is the best type of foreign aid. And it is good for American consumers and investors.

The Political Economy of Protectionism

by Thomas J. DiLorenzo

Disagreements among economists are legendary, but they are largely of one mind on the issue of free trade. Evidence of this is a recent survey of the current and past presidents of the American Economic Association—the voice of mainstream economics. The survey found these prominent economists all strongly in favor of free trade, and concluded that "an economist who argues for restricting trade is almost as common today as a physician who favors leeching patients."[1]

Mainstream economic thinking on free trade knows no ideological boundaries. Conservative economists Milton and Rose Friedman, for example, write that "ever since Adam Smith there has been virtual unanimity among economists . . . that international free trade is in the best interest of the trading countries and the world."[2] Liberal economist Paul Samuelson concurs: "Free trade promotes a mutually profitable regional division of labor, greatly enhances the potential real national product of all nations, and makes possible higher standards of living all over the globe."[3]

The case for free trade is not based on any stylized economic theories of "perfect competition," "general equilibrium," or "partial equilibrium." After all, Adam Smith is history's most forceful and articulate defender of free trade, and he never heard of any of those theories. Rather, the case for free trade is based on the virtues of voluntary exchange, the division of labor, and individual freedom.

As long as trade is voluntary, both trading partners unequivocally benefit; otherwise they wouldn't trade. The purchase of a shirt, for instance, demonstrates that the purchaser values the shirt more than the money spent on it. The seller, on the other hand, values the money more than the shirt. Thus, both are better off because of the sale. Moreover, it doesn't matter whether the shirt salesman is from the United States or Hong Kong (or anywhere else). Voluntary exchange is always mutually beneficial.

Free trade expands consumer choice and gives businesses incentives to improve product quality and to cut costs. By increasing the sup-

---

Dr. DiLorenzo is a professor of economics at Loyola College in Baltimore, Maryland. This article was originally published in the July 1988 issue of *The Freeman*.

ply of goods, international competition helps hold down prices and restrains internal monopolies. The "Big Three" automakers, for instance, may *wish* to monopolize the automobile market, but they are unable to because of foreign competition. About 75 percent of all domestic manufacturing industries now face some international competition, which helps keep their competitive feet to the fire. Thus, the case for free trade is the case for competition, higher quality goods, economic growth, and lower prices. By contrast, the case for protectionism is the case for monopoly, lower quality goods, economic stagnation, and higher prices.

The costs of protectionism to consumers are enormous. According to very conservative estimates, protectionism costs American consumers over $60 billion per year—more than $1,000 annually for a family of four.[4] Thanks to protectionism, for example, it costs about $2,500 more to buy a Japanese-made car than it otherwise would.

Free trade increases the wealth (and employment opportunities) of all nations by allowing them to capitalize on their comparative advantages in production. For example, the United States has a comparative advantage in the production of food because of its vast, fertile land and superior agricultural technology and labor. Saudi Arabia, on the other hand, does not have land that is well suited to agriculture. Although Saudi Arabia conceivably could undertake massive irrigation to become self-sufficient in food production, it is more economical for the Saudis to sell what they *do* have a comparative advantage in—oil—and then purchase much of their food from the United States and elsewhere. Similarly, the United States could become self-sufficient in petroleum by squeezing more oil out of shale rock and tar sands. But that would be much more costly than if the U.S. continued to purchase some of its oil from Saudi Arabia and elsewhere. Trade between the United States and Saudi Arabia, or any other two countries, improves the standard of living in each.

Ethical Aspects of Free Trade

Protectionism is not only economically inefficient, it is also inherently unjust. It is the equivalent of a regressive tax, placing the heaviest burden on those who can least afford it. For example, because of import restraints in the footwear industry, shoes are more expensive. This imposes a proportionately larger burden on the family that has an income of only $15,000 per year than on the family that has an income of, say, $75,000 per year. Moreover, the beneficiaries of protectionism are often more affluent than those who bear the costs. Wages in the heavily protected auto industry are about 80 percent higher than the average wage in U.S. manufacturing. The chairman of the Chrysler Corporation was paid $28 million in 1987, thanks partly to protectionism. And, perversely, by driving up the price of automobiles, protectionism has benefited the owners, managers, and workers of the *Japanese* automobile industry at the expense of American consumers. Protectionism, in other words, is welfare for the well-to-do.

Protectionism also conflicts with the humanitarian goals of foreign development aid. The U.S. government spends billions of dollars annually in foreign aid to developing countries. Many of these programs are themselves counterproductive because they simply subsidize governmental bureaucracies in the recipient countries. But what good does it do to try to assist these countries if we block them from the biggest market in the world for their goods? Protectionism stifles economic growth in the developing countries, leaving them even more dependent upon U.S. government handouts.

Why Protectionism?

Despite the powerful case for free trade, both the United States and the rest of the world are highly protectionist, and always have been. This is because free trade benefits the general public, whereas protectionism benefits a relatively small group of special interests. The general public is neither well organized nor well informed politically, but the special interests are. This political imbalance was recognized by Adam Smith over 200 years ago when he wrote in *The Wealth of Nations* that

> To expect, indeed, that the freedom of trade should ever be entirely restored in Great Britain, is as absurd as to expect that an Oceana or Utopia should ever be established in it. Not only the prejudices of the public, but what is much more unconquerable, the private interests of many individuals, irresistibly oppose it. . . . The member of parliament who supports every proposal for strengthening this monopoly, is sure to acquire not only the reputation of understanding trade, but great popularity and influence with an order of men whose numbers and wealth render them of great importance. If he opposes them, on the contrary, and still more if he has authority enough to be able to thwart them, neither the most acknowledged probity, nor the highest rank, nor the greatest public services can pro-

tect him from the most infamous abuse and detraction, from personal insults, nor sometimes from real danger, arising from the insolent outrage of furious and disappointed monopolists.[5]

The political pressures to grant monopolistic privileges are so strong that even political figures who spend their careers speaking in favor of free trade quickly cave in to protectionist pressures once in office. U.S. Treasury Secretary James Baker recently boasted, for example, that "President Reagan has granted more import relief to U.S. industry than any of his predecessors in more than half a century."[6] Unfortunately, the Democratic party is not very different. "There is no strong supporter of a free and open trading system," complained Hobart Rowan of the *Washington Post*, "among the seven declared Democratic [1988 Presidential] candidates."[7]

Voters might be expected to oppose policies that stifle economic growth and redistribute income from poor to rich. But public opposition to protectionism is not very strong, explains economist Mancur Olson, because "the typical citizen is usually 'rationally ignorant' about public affairs."[8] That is, the typical citizen spends most of his or her time worrying about personal matters and not economic policy. To add to the confusion, much of the information that citizens do receive about public policy is self-serving and biased information disseminated by special-interest lobbyists. As economist Gordon Tullock has written:

> Special interest groups normally have an interest in diminishing the information of the average voter. If they can sell him some false tale which supports their particular effort to rob the treasury, it pays. They have resources and normally make efforts to produce this kind of misinformation. But that would not work if the voter had a strong motive to learn the truth.[9]

For decades monopolists and potential monopolists have crafted hundreds of myths about free trade and protectionism. The following are just a few examples of misinformation about protectionism.

Protectionism Myths

Myth #1: *Imports (and trade deficits) are bad; exports (and trade surpluses) are good.*

The international trade deficit has been of concern to Congress in recent years, and has been a primary "justification" for protection. But the notion that importing more than we export is necessarily bad ignores some elementary economic principles. First, imports are our *gain* from trade. The more material goods—the more trade—the better. Remember, *all* trade is mutually beneficial.

How trade-deficit statistics can give misleading impressions of economic health is illustrated by the analogy between domestic and international trade. Most citizens probably run a trade deficit with their grocers. But who would argue that a balance of trade between consumers and grocers is necessarily desirable? A government-mandated trade balance—whether for domestic or international trade—would make both trading partners worse off. Furthermore, the notion that, say, Taiwan, with a population of 20 million, should buy as many goods from the United States as 230 million American consumers purchase from Taiwan is absurd. The balance of trade argument is just another weak excuse for monopolistic trade restrictions.

Myth #2: *Being a "debtor nation" is economically harmful.*

Being a debtor nation means that foreigners invest more in the United States than U.S. citizens invest abroad. Debtor nation status is not necessarily a cause for alarm, however, since foreign investment in the United States can be beneficial. For example, there are many obvious benefits from Tennessee's new Nissan plant and the 50 other Japanese companies located in that state. These new companies provide jobs, make American industry more competitive, and stimulate economic growth. The United States has been a debtor nation throughout most of its history, including the period from 1787 to 1920, when the nation experienced the most rapid economic growth in world history up to that time.

Alarm over becoming a debtor nation is illogical and contradictory. On the one hand, protectionists complain that too much money is leaving the country (we're importing more than we're exporting). Then, when the same money returns to the United States in the form of foreign investment, they complain that too much money is coming *into* the country. The protectionists cannot have it both ways. They are grasping at straws to justify monopolistic privileges.

Myth #3: *Imports are destroying American jobs.*

Like all long-lasting myths, this one has a grain of truth. If more American consumers buy Japanese rather than American-made cars, it may threaten some American jobs. Efforts should be (and are) made to ease the transition of those who become temporarily unemployed, but protectionism would only cause even more unemployment.

Free trade *creates* jobs by reducing prices, leaving more money in the pockets of consumers. Increased consumer spending in turn will stimulate production *and employment* throughout the economy. By contrast, higher prices in a protected industry will cause consumers to cut back on their purchases, which will result in *less* employment in that industry.

Also, the dollars that Americans pay for foreign-made goods eventually are respent in the United States, which creates even more jobs. Foreigners have no use for dollars per se. They must either spend them in the United States or sell them to someone who will.

Protectionism may *temporarily* "save" jobs in one industry, but it usually destroys even more jobs elsewhere. For example, because of protectionism in the steel industry, American automakers are estimated to pay as much as $500 more per car for steel than Japanese automakers. Higher prices for American-made cars will cost domestic automakers business and cause them to lay off workers. Thus, protectionism in the steel industry creates unemployment in steel-using industries.

It is particularly telling that in recent years, as the trade deficit has grown, so has employment in the U.S. economy. More than 13 million new jobs were created between 1982 and 1988 as the unemployment rate dropped from nearly 11 percent to less then 6 percent of the labor force. In contrast, we had a trade *surplus* throughout the 1970s when unemployment rose steadily.

Myth #4: *Because of international competition, the U.S. manufacturing sector is declining.*

Protectionists have claimed that the U.S. economy is "deindustrializing" because of the alleged failure of American manufacturers to compete in international markets. But the deindustrialization theory is a hoax. Manufacturing output as a percentage of GNP is about 24 percent today, compared to 25 percent in 1950.[10] Moreover, manufacturing output *and employment* are at their highest levels ever. The *composition* of employment and output has changed, as it always does in a dynamic, growing economy. Economic growth always creates many dislocations. Overall, however, the U.S. manufacturing sector is not "deindustrializing."

Myth #5: *Because of international competition, many newly created jobs are low-paying, "dead-end" jobs.*

One congressman claimed that "50 percent of the 13 million new jobs [created between 1982 and 1987] are dead-end—paying $7,400 a year or less. We're trading good manufacturing jobs for low-pay service jobs."[11] The congressman asserted that international trade is "impoverishing America," and has introduced protectionist legislation to thwart this perceived trend.

The U.S. Department of Labor recently examined these claims in great detail and found the reality to be much different from the congressman's rhetoric. Of the 13 million new jobs created between 1982 and 1987, 59 percent were in the *highest-wage* category as classified by the Labor Department. Only 7 percent of the new jobs were minimum-wage jobs paying $7,400 per year or less.[12]

Myth #6: *Cheap foreign labor is an unfair advantage.*
It is often said that if, say, textile workers in Singapore are paid only $1 per hour, American industry cannot possibly compete, given that American textile workers are paid more than $10 per hour. Protection is supposedly needed if the domestic textile industry is to survive.

This argument may appear compelling at first, but it ignores several important facts. First, if the productivity of American workers is ten times as high as in Singapore (because of superior capital, technology, and training), then higher American wages are not a disadvantage.

Second, the idea that low wages "explain" international trade patterns is illogical. If it were true, the United States would export almost nothing, since U.S. wages are higher than almost everywhere else in the world across the board. What determines a nation's comparative advantage in international trade is the *total* amount of resources it must use to produce a given product, not just the labor. Many low-wage countries import U.S. goods because we have a comparative advantage in producing those goods despite our higher wages. Moreover, low-wage countries *must* eventually import goods from the United States because there is nothing else they can do with the dollars they receive from their American sales.

Finally, it isn't clear why it is "unfair" for American consumers to enjoy lower-priced and/or higher-quality goods produced overseas by low-wage (or other) countries.

Myth #7: *Protection is necessary to counteract "dumping."*
So-called dumping occurs when foreign manufacturers sell products in the United States that supposedly are priced below the price at which they are sold in the home market. There are numerous laws that prohibit dumping on the grounds that it is unfair competition.

But there are also sound economic reasons for such business practices. Temporarily charging prices that are below cost is a common *com-*

petitive business practice. For example, newly established pizza parlors typically offer "two for the price of one" specials as an inducement to consumers to try out their product. The losses incurred during the sales are considered an investment that will yield future sales by generating a clientele. Lower prices always benefit consumers, but we seldom charge the local pizza parlor with "dumping." Perhaps this is because consumers can plainly see the benefits of such competition.

In November 1987, the U.S. Commerce Department ruled that "Japanese companies violated international trade laws by failing to increase their prices to match the sharp rise in the value of the yen."[13] With the rise in the value of the yen, Japanese goods sold in the United States became relatively more expensive. The Japanese producers responded by cutting their costs, prices, and profit margins to remain competitive, to the great satisfaction of American consumers. According to the Commerce Department, Japanese export prices declined by 23 percent between 1985 and 1987. Unfortunately, the protectionist Reagan administration is opposed to such price cutting.

Dumping is often said to occur because foreign governments subsidize some of their manufacturers, which allows the companies to underprice American firms. These policies may be misguided, but there is no reason why American consumers should be punished for the shortsighted policies of foreign governments. Such subsidies constitute a "gift" from foreign taxpayers to American consumers and may be thought of as foreign aid in reverse. Moreover, the extent to which this subsidization takes place has been greatly exaggerated. In Japan, for instance, the amount of assistance given to Japanese manufacturers by the Japan Development Bank has amounted to less than one percent of gross domestic investment, and most of that has gone into the agricultural sector.

Dumping is also objected to on the grounds that it is a means of monopolizing American industries by driving out the competition with low prices. There have been no documented examples of such monopolization, however, and for good reason. Any manufacturer who charged monopolistic prices would face fierce international (and domestic) competition that would quickly dissipate any monopoly power. Businesses that charge their international competitors with dumping are simply unwilling to charge prices that are as low as their rivals'.

Myth #8: *Temporary protection is needed to "buy time" and adjust to the competition.*

Temporary trade relief is like being a little bit pregnant. The textile industry, for example, was given "temporary" trade relief 25 years ago and is still being "relieved." This rationale admits that protectionism is a bad idea, which is why it is labeled as only temporary. However, it is bound to make things worse for the industry, not better.

By reducing competitive pressures, protectionism tends to stifle innovation. Businesses are less prone to invest in engineering and technology when profits can be earned just as easily by lobbying for protection.

There is much evidence, moreover, that "temporary" protection does not revitalize industries, and probably is even counterproductive. The federal government's Congressional Budget Office studied protectionism in the textile, steel, footwear, and automobile industries, and concluded that "in none of the cases studied did protection . . . revitalize the affected industry. . . . Protection has not substantially improved the ability of domestic firms to compete with foreign producers."[14] The study showed that investment often *declines* during periods of protection, which causes the protected industries to fall even farther behind the competition. Such evidence explains why a closely related protectionist argument—the military might argument—is also fiction. Specifically, if an industry is important to national defense, it supposedly should be protected from international competition. But since protection saps incentives for innovation, resulting in lower-quality and higher-priced goods, it will *weaken* the national defense by weakening industries that the military relies upon.

Myth #9: *We should restore a "level playing field" by erecting trade barriers against countries that have trade barriers against us.*

This is a "cutting off our nose to spite our face" strategy. If foreign governments are foolish enough to harm their own citizens by erecting trade barriers, it is unfortunate for those citizens. But there are no sound reasons why American consumers should be penalized for the ill-conceived trade policies of foreign governments.

Furthermore, trade retaliation would be hypocritical, since American trade restrictions on foreign imports are often much greater than foreign restrictions on American imports. The American auto parts supply industry, for example, is currently lobbying for protection on the grounds of "unfair competition" from Japanese auto parts suppliers. The hypocrisy of this claim stems from the fact that there are no Japanese government-imposed barriers to importing American auto parts into Japan, but Japanese parts producers must pay American tariffs when exporting to the United States.

Trade retaliation can be a very dangerous political game. The

Smoot-Hawley Tariff of 1930 spawned an international trade war that helped precipitate the Great Depression. Dozens of countries responded to the Smoot-Hawley Tariff by erecting trade barriers for American-made goods. Consequently, the value of imports in the 75 most active trading countries fell from over $3 billion in 1929 to about $1 billion by 1932, driving the world economy into a depression.[15]

Trade retaliation is inherently counterproductive. Reducing the flow of dollars from the United States means that foreigners will have fewer dollars to spend there, which eventually will harm American export industries. American exports generally fall once imports are reduced. Consequently, employment in export-related industries, which account for as much as one-fifth of all employment in the United States, will fall.[16]

Myth #10: *Protectionism benefits union members.*

This is probably true in the short run, but certainly not in the long run. Because of protectionism in such industries as steel, automobiles, textiles, and footwear, unions once prospered by imposing featherbedding rules and by bargaining for supra-competitive wages. As long as international competition was not very effective, raising wages while reducing productivity was feasible. However, international competition eventually seeped in, as it inevitably does, and American industries found themselves at a severe competitive disadvantage. They lost market share, laid off thousands of workers, and union membership declined dramatically. Thus, protectionism may have helped unions in the short run, but is a main cause of their current malaise. It is no coincidence that some of America's most lethargic unionized industries—steel, automobiles, footwear, rubber, textiles—are also among the most heavily protected.

Conclusions

In sum, a dynamic economy is essential for economic growth and job creation, and protectionism only hinders the necessary adaptations to economic change. As Nobel Laureate Friedrich Hayek has written, the benefits of competition and economic growth

> are the results of such changes, and will be maintained only if the changes are allowed to continue. But every change of this kind will hurt some organized interests; and the preservation of the market order will therefore depend on those interests not being able to prevent what they dislike. . . . [T]his general interest will be satisfied only if the principle is recognized that each

has to submit to changes when circumstances nobody can control determine that he is the one who is placed under such a necessity.[17]

Protectionism may provide some short-term benefits to a small number of special interests, but at much greater costs to the rest of society. Restraints on international trade are inefficient, inequitable, and counterproductive, and should not be imposed.

1. Julian Simon and Robert Crandall, "Singular Economic Response," *Washington Times*, September 10, 1987, p. F-1.

2. Milton and Rose Friedman, *Free to Choose* (New York: Harcourt Brace Jovanovich, 1979), p. 39.

3. Paul Samuelson, *Economics* (New York: Macmillan, 1976), p. 692.

4. Michael C. Munger, "The Costs of Protectionism," *Challenge*, January/February 1984, pp. 54- 58.

5. Adam Smith, *The Wealth of Nations* (Indianapolis: Liberty Classics, 1981), p. 471.

6. Lindley Clark, "Reaganomics Reassessed," *Wall Street Journal*, September 24, 1987, p. 26.

7. Hobart Rowan, "Free-Trade Coalition Fades," *Washington Post*, September 20, 1987, p. H- 1.

8. Mancur Olson, *The Rise and Decline of Nations* (New Haven: Yale University Press, 1982), p. 26.

9. Gordon Tullock, *Welfare for the Well-to-Do* (Dallas: The Fisher Institute, 1983), p. 71.

10. See U.S. Department of Commerce, Bureau of the Census, *Statistical Abstract of the U.S.* (Washington, D.C.: U.S. Government Printing Office, various years).

11. Warren Brookes, "The Myth That Won't Die," *Washington Times*, September 7, 1987, p. D-1.

12. Brookes, p. D-1.

13. Stuart Auerbach, "Japanese Companies Violated Trade Laws," *Washington Post*, November 20, 1987, p. D-1.

14. Congressional Budget Office, *Has Trade Protection Revitalized Domestic Industries?* (Washington, D.C.: CBO, November 1986), p. 97.

15. Robert Bartley, "1929 and All That," *Wall Street Journal*, November 24, 1987, p. 28.

16. "Export-Dependent Manufacturing Employment," Washington, D.C.: U.S. Trade Representative, 1984.

17. F.A. Hayek, *Law, Legislation, and Liberty*, vol. 3 (Chicago: University of Chicago Press, 1976), p. 94.

Protectionism and Unemployment

by Hans F. Sennholz

There is a disturbing thing about foreign affairs: they are foreign. They do not conform to the world we admire, which is our own. Foreign matters are viewed with suspicion, yea, even dislike and contempt. Protectionism, which proposes to use the authority of government and its instruments of coercion to restrict trade with foreigners, builds on this psychological foundation.

In the minds of many people the ancient association of foreigner with enemy still lingers. Foreigners are blamed for all kinds of evil, real and imagined. They are censured for being inscrutable and unpredictable in their trade relations, engaging in ruthless competition, gouging their trade partners through prices too high or too low, exploiting their workers through sweatshop wages and conditions. But above all, trade with foreigners is believed to be most disruptive to commerce and industry, ever changing in composition and structure, requiring painful readjustment.

Protectionists offer instant gains through removal of foreign competition and protection from the pains of readjustment. Appealing to people who do not care to change and others who uphold domestic changes, but are set at odds with foreign changes, they promise peace and profit through legislation, regulation and the use of police power. But despite all the opposition to change, the world is a scene of changes. Today is not yesterday. We ourselves change as do our thoughts and works. Change may be painful, yet ever needful.

In our economic lives we may face important changes that require our attention and adjustment. The tastes, habits, choices, and preferences of consumers may change, which may dictate production adjustments. The worldwide pattern of division of labor may change, which affects the structure of trade and commerce. The costs of production may change either here or abroad, which may create competitive advantages or disadvantages. There may be a never-ending sequence

Dr. Sennholz, formerly Chairman of the Department of Economics at Grove City College, now serves as President of The Foundation for Economic Education in Irvington-on-Hudson, New York. He is a noted writer and lecturer on economic, political, and monetary affairs. This article was originally published in the March 1985 issue of *The Freeman*.

of changes in labor costs, capital costs, material costs, transportation costs, government costs, and many other costs.

Man faces changes in international trade and commerce to which he must adjust. After all, foreign trade is merely an extension of domestic trade, which is a corollary from the principles of division of labor. Cooperation and specialization bring the same kinds of benefits to all people regardless of race, religion, or nationality. They make human labor more productive through exchange rather than direct production. If trade between the people in California, Texas, Florida, and Maine is advantageous, it follows that free trade between people in Guatemala and Mexico, or Canada and Costa Rica may also be advantageous.[1]

Protectionism, Old and New

Most of the arguments in favor of restriction stem from the distant past. Many are crudely mercantilistic; they favor exports and oppose imports. Mercantilists are concerned about an unfavorable balance of trade which, they believe, inflicts loss and waste. In the past they restricted imports and promoted exports in order to bring money into the country. The neo-mercantilists of our time favor exports for bringing in jobs and profits, and oppose imports for taking them out.

Mercantilistic notions, although discarded by most economists, live on regardless of the criticism that is levied against them. Businessmen remember them when they are encountering difficulties and calling on government, pleading protection from foreign competitors. The agents of labor retreat to the armory of mercantilism when they are enmeshed in depression and unemployment. And government officials may plead the case for mercantilism when they impose their regulations and controls on foreign trade and commerce, or grant subsidies, set rates, or gather information to promote exports and limit imports. They all hold to the persistent belief that exports are especially beneficial and praiseworthy, and imports *ipso facto* harmful.

The recrudescence of mercantilism dates back to the early part of this century, and came to a head during the 1930s. Guided by a spirit of nationalism it sought national self-sufficiency through restrictive tariffs, import quotas, and exchange restrictions. It differed from the older mercantilism in that it received strength and support from a philosophy of militant nationalism and economic welfarism. It was associated with comprehensive central planning by powerful governments engaging in economic warfare and military struggle.

The neo-mercantilism of the 1970s and 1980s differs from the 1930s' version in two important respects: it is devoid of the blatant nationalism of the first half of the century and its beggar-my-neighbor attitude; but it is saturated with the notions and doctrines of full employment by government fiat. Mindful of international sensibilities, it resorts to more subtle but equally deadly restrictions, to subsidies rather than tariffs and quotas. It does not aim at economic autarky for nationalistic ends, but at income and employment in favored industries. It does not spring from international confrontation, but from an inter-industry conflict that pits some industries against all others.

In the American steel industry, for example, capital and labor together conspire to restrict imports in order to boost corporate earnings and labor benefits. Embarrassed by the low rates of production and the high rates of unemployment, they both call on government to restrain competition in any shape or form. They both plead as ardently for minimum-wage legislation, which is designed to handicap other industries, as they argue forcefully against the competition of foreigners. For labor unions especially, government protection is of crucial importance. After all, to win substantial boosts in wages and benefits and subsequently suffer from staggering unemployment is casting serious doubt on the rationale of unionism.

Workers' Rights Movements in Europe and the U.S.A.

The labor movement in the United States closely resembles the workers' rights movements in the European welfare states. They both expound the doctrine that workers have an inherent right to a job, in their particular industry, at their present location and at rates of pay that exceed the market rates. To secure their right, government is expected to restrain foreign competition in any possible way and, if needed, subsidize both labor and capital.[2] In this respect, protectionism is a symptom of relatively weak national governments catering to powerful domestic interest groups, especially labor.

Protectionism also draws strength and support from the Keynesian mandate that government is responsible for full employment and that it must use its fiscal powers in a contracyclical manner. Such use of powers for purposes of market intervention may necessitate protection from foreign competition. After all, Keynesian recipes are national recipes that differ from those for world markets and international division of labor.

When Keynesian efforts succeed in raising goods prices, domestic producers suffer in competitiveness at home and abroad. Threatened by foreign competition, they may call for protection through import restrictions. When Keynesian efforts fail to achieve full employment the

Keynesian planners further express their faith in government intervention as they turn to protectionist measures. The failure of Keynesianism
breeds protectionism. Many Keynesians are joining the workers' rights
movement and lending new luster to the promises of protection.[3]

Old Notions in New Garb

The labor movement and its Keynesian allies like to parade as
champions of the less-developed countries. They are quick to disburse
foreign aid to any and all applicants and finance their schemes of government enterprise. But many immediately draw the line when jobs are
"exported" for the benefit of foreigners. They are dead set against capital and labor mobility that permits capital to move to less-developed
countries and labor to more productive countries.[4] In all such matters
they plead for restrictions that are said to bestow net benefits on society.

Man often errs through selfishness. Economic restrictions always
benefit some people at the expense of others, and inflict net losses on
society. Protectionists do not look beyond the range of direct involve-
ment and dealing. American steel workers may see only their own
wages and benefits which trade restrictions are meant to protect. They
point at the market of goods and services catering to the steel industry
in general and to steel workers in particular, and warn of dire consequences if these markets be permitted to decline. They completely
ignore all other consequences and ramifications of restrictions, and
refuse to admit that any favor bestowed on the steel industry is a disfa-
vor to all others. Domestic trade is substituted for foreign trade, and
domestic steel for foreign steel. The quantity of steel offered in
exchange for other goods is reduced, which makes economic society
universally poorer. The sellers of food, clothing, housing, education,
and the like receive less steel in exchange for their goods and services.
They would have been better off if they had been permitted to trade
with foreign steel makers.

The protection argument for full employment is similar to that for
net benefits. To working people it seems self-evident that import restrictions add to the demand for labor, and that steel and automobile quotas
provide employment for steel and auto workers. Such evidence, unfortunately, is rather shallow and deceptive; it fails to consider other effects
that are bound to follow. Import restrictions are restraints imposed by
politicians and enforced by the apparatus of coercion, the courts and
police. They constitute the use of brute force against people who volun-
tarily and peacefully are engaged in international exchange, in order to
force them to act in a way they would not act if they were free.

Methods of Restriction Are Widely Available

The methods of restriction may vary greatly, from monetary exactions to outright confiscation of private property; they are highly effective in setting bounds to human action. When trade restrictions are imposed, the protected industry may temporarily enjoy special gains, which may cause it to expand and hire more labor, or retain more labor than it otherwise would. But this extra demand for labor, for instance, steel labor, is marred by a simultaneous decline in the demand for other labor, e.g., for food, clothing, housing. After all, the extra money spent on steel and steel products cannot be spent on other products, and the economic resources employed in the production of steel cannot be employed in other production. And the labor needed for the production of steel is no longer available for the production of food, clothing, housing, and so on.

At this point, protectionists are quick to object that there is always unemployed labor and capital waiting to be called provided government lends a helping hand by restraining foreign competition. They point at mass unemployment in basic industries, such as steel, autos, mining, and transportation, and demand immediate correction through protection.

Unemployment undoubtedly is a great social evil that concerns us all. It is an economic phenomenon of loss and waste that harms not only the jobless but also their fellow workers who are forced to support them. In time it tends to turn into a political issue that breeds confrontation and conflict. To alleviate the evils of unemployment becomes an important political task. But it also raises the basic question of the suitability of the policies that are to create employment. In particular, it poses the question: Can tariff barriers and other trade restrictions raise the demand for labor and alleviate the evils of unemployment?

Unemployment is a cost and wage phenomenon; foreign trade is exchange by individuals separated by political boundaries. The former is a manifestation of the law of price, which rests on the valuations by all members of society; the latter pertains to the scope of the division of labor which man is willing to practice. This scope does affect goods prices, including the price of labor. Improvements in the division of labor generally raise labor productivity and wage rates; deterioration reduces them. When government imposes trade restrictions it reduces the marginal productivity of labor and thereby lowers wage rates. If, in this situation, workers should refuse to suffer wage cuts, they are inviting mass unemployment. When seen in this light, trade barriers are effective instruments for causing unemployment.

In many respects production restrictions and trade barriers are like natural obstacles that thwart human effort and impair man's productivity. They both may increase the demand for specific labor. Destruction of housing by war, flood, earthquake or fire increases the demand for housing material and construction labor. But it also reduces the demand for a myriad of other goods which the destruction victims now must forgo. Similarly, import restrictions on steel may boost the demand for domestic steel, but they also reduce the demand for other goods which the restriction victims, that is, consumers must forgo. Steel producers and their workers may benefit from the new barriers; but the producers and workers in all other industries are likely to suffer losses.

Many workingmen welcome trade restrictions in the same way as they greet the breakdown and destruction of labor-saving tools and appliances. They are aware of the demand for their particular kind of labor and know how to increase it through protection and elimination of labor-saving tools. They apply the particular to the general and conclude that protection provides employment and destruction creates jobs. Unfortunately, they fail to see that both, restriction and destruction, are bound to reduce the marginal productivity of labor throughout the labor market. If, in this situation, affected workers should resist a prompt reduction of wage rates, which organized labor is likely to support with conviction and force, they face mass unemployment. After all, unemployment always visits that labor the cost of which exceeds its productivity.

Trade Restrictions Offer Temporary Relief

Trade restrictions may temporarily create new employment opportunities for a protected industry while other industries are forced to contract. But even in the protected industry they do not provide long-term employment, as the root causes of unemployment continue to be at work. The basic industries suffering from stagnation and unemployment generally are unionized industries with wages and benefits far in excess of nonunion market compensation. Labor unions enforce their rates through restriction of labor competition; the basic effect is unemployment. They apply their unrelenting pressures until they are enmeshed in depression and unemployment. To come to their rescue and grant them protection from foreign competition is to invite new restriction and more unemployment.

In a profound study, M. Kreinin recently demonstrated that labor compensation in the American automobile industry, in 1982, amounted to some 165 percent of that in all manufactures. To become competitive with Japanese car makers, he concluded, United Auto Workers' compensation would have to fall by 24 percent, which would leave their compensation still 25 percent above the U.S. manufacturing average. Similarly, in iron and steel production workers' wages and benefits amount to 189 percent of those in all manufactures. To restore competitiveness with Japan they would have to fall by 39 percent, which would leave their compensation still 15 percent above the U.S. manufacturing average.[5] But no such solution to the chronic unemployment in the steel and auto industries is under consideration. Instead, their spokesmen are clamoring ever louder for protection from "unfair" foreign competition.

Trade barriers destroy more jobs than they create. And yet, they have retained their popularity because most workers are convinced that they safeguard wage rates from the competition of low-cost labor. Without trade barriers, many Americans believe, foreign products made by cheap labor would flood the markets and force American labor to suffer substantial wage cuts or face unemployment. Free trade is said to be advantageous only between countries that have similar wage rates and similar standards of living, but thought to be harmful to people with high wages trading with people earning less. Americans and Canadians can trade with each other because they are similar in income and living conditions; but they must not trade with Mexicans who engage in unfair pauper-labor competition and cause U.S. living conditions to fall.

There are few arguments in favor of protection that are more popular and yet so specious and fallacious. When carried to its logical conclusion the wage-rate argument bars all trade across political boundaries as no two countries are identical in labor productivity and income. U.S. wage rates are generally higher than Canadian rates, which would call for American government protection from low-cost labor competition in Canada. Labor conditions may differ from state to state, yea, from community to community. Wage rates in New York state are generally higher than in Maine and Mississippi, which would call for government intervention in favor of labor in New York.

Differences in Productivity and Income Lead to Trade

In freedom, differences in labor productivity and income lead to exchanges of goods and services. As individual inequality brings forth man's division of labor so does his inequality in national productivity and output lead to international division of labor and goods exchanges. Adam Smith already taught that it is advantageous for a country to specialize in the production of those goods in which it has a cost advantage. David Ricardo added the law of comparative cost according to which it also is advantageous to a country to specialize in those items in which it has a comparative advantage.

To reap the advantages of an international division of labor a country may concentrate on production with greatest comparative advantage, importing even some items that can be produced at lower cost at home than abroad.[6] Improvements in international division of labor raise labor productivity and, wherever institutional restrictions have created unemployment, may actually lift some labor over the threshold of employability and thereby create jobs.

The competitive position of an industry may depend on the capital-labor composition of the product. A labor-intensive product, such as a hand-embroidered tablecloth, may be manufactured most advantageously in a low-wage country. A capital-intensive product requiring the application of large sums of capital may be manufactured most efficiently in the country with the largest per capita supply of capital and lowest interest rates. The manufacturers of Hong Kong, where wage rates are rather low when compared with U.S. standards, have a clear advantage in the production of hand-embroidery; U.S. manufacturers who benefit from efficient capital markets and relatively low capital costs have a clear cost advantage in the manufacture of capital-intensive products, for instance, $50-million airplanes.

Trade advantages may change when factor costs change. Where capital is being formed and made available at ever lower interest cost, capital-intensive industries are likely to prosper and expand. Where society and its political institutions consume productive capital, the industries can be expected to contract and discharge labor. When Toyota may secure capital for modernization and expansion at 7 percent while General Motors is forced to pay 14 percent in a depleted capital market, it becomes rather obvious that Toyota will continue to expand and employ more labor while GM must be expected to contract and dismiss some labor.

Many Factors Affect the Degree of Competition

The costs of capital and labor are merely two of many factors that determine the competitiveness of an industry. There are many other factors such as the methods of production and the state of technology, transportation costs for materials and supplies and for products to their markets, government regulation, taxation, environmental costs and other institutional costs. A change of any one, at home or abroad, may materially alter the competitive position of an industry. The formation of capital per head of the population generally raises labor productivity and reduces unemployment; the consumption of capital lowers labor productivity and depresses wage rates. Where labor resists the reduction and insists on remuneration that exceeds market rates, it invites mass unemployment.

It is significant that governments generally do not protect industries with relatively low rates of productivity and wages, industries with a great deal of unskilled labor. In the United States these industries are forced to labor under great difficulties created by minimum wage legislation. The U.S. government, under the influence of powerful labor interests, apparently prefers foreign imports from low-wage countries such as Korea, Hong Kong, and Taiwan over domestic production in the South and especially Puerto Rico. But it is granting considerable protection to industries that are known to pay the highest wage rates in the world.

The U.S. government is guided by the doctrine of "no injury," which brought into being the "escape clause" where injury is reported, and the "peril points" below which import duties must not be reduced. Protectionism is visible in the trade adjustment assistance granted to workers, in agreements with foreign exporters, the establishment of the International Trade Commission, and other concessions granted to interests with congressional clout. Protectionism springs ever anew from the efforts of "distributional coalitions," which use political power to restrict competition and output.

U.S.-Japanese Trade Relations

Protectionists in the United States spend a great deal of time and effort worrying and complaining about Japanese trade practices. They focus their concern on Japan with which the United States is running a huge deficit in its merchandise trade account. According to the Council of Economic Advisers *Annual Report,* the 1976–83 deficit amounted to some $95 billion primarily as a result of Japanese sales of textiles, television sets, automobiles, motorcycles, radios, photographic equipment, video tape recorders, watches, machine tools, and steel.[7] A *Business Week* cover story calls it "America's Hidden Problem: The Huge Trade Deficit is Sapping Growth and Exporting Jobs." (August 29, 1983)

American complaints about Japanese trade practices may have some merit, but they do not lead to the conclusions drawn by *Business Week* and other protectionists. They do not justify making Japan the "whipping boy" for trade deficits for which the U.S. government is primarily responsible. After all, it is an undeniable fact that U.S. trade restrictions completely bar Japanese buyers from important U.S. markets and thereby inflict visible losses not only on American producers but also on the Japanese people as consumers. Trade deficits may spring from a number of causes among which disruptive policies conducted by the U.S. government must not be overlooked.

There is transcendent power in example. U.S. leadership in international policy-making may be slipping because the U.S. example is unconvincing. The United States surely is no free-trade country; the U.S. government has entered into international trade agreements on cocoa, coffee, rubber, sugar, and tea. It has built trigger price mechanisms in steel and imposed "voluntary" quotas on autos and textiles. The maritime industry represented by seamen's unions and unionized domestic shipbuilders has managed to obtain legislation that forces Alaskan oil producers to ship their products in high-cost U.S. tankers to uneconomic destinations in the United States. The legislation hit hard at Japanese levels of living by cutting the Japanese people off from Alaskan crude oil. It is estimated that, under free-trade conditions, they could be expected to buy some $15 billion annually, which alone would eliminate the merchandise trade deficit with Japan.[8]

The Japanese people must import almost all of their oil. In a free world unhampered by trade barriers Alaskan producers would be their least-cost suppliers. In the political world of trade restrictions special interests in the United States deny them access to the Alaskan market. The Trans-Alaska Pipeline Authorization Act of 1973 and the 1977 and 1979 amendments to the Export Administration Act virtually shut the Alaskan door to foreigners and forced them to seek supplies in far-distant Arabian and African markets. It is obvious that transport charges per barrel of Saudi oil are substantially higher than for Alaskan oil, and materially higher for Alaskan oil shipped to the West Coast and the Gulf Coast than for oil shipped to Japan.

Higher Shipping Costs

The higher transportation costs visibly raise total cost, which increases world prices, reduces labor productivity and impairs economic well-being. But a few American seamen and shipbuilders are enjoying a windfall through trade disruption. It is estimated that more than 90 percent of U.S. shipping capacity, measured in deadweight tonnage, and probably more than half of all American seamen serve to carry oil from Alaska to U.S. ports.[9]

Notions of full employment and favors to organized labor have led the U.S. government to impose an embargo not only on the shipment of Alaskan crude but also on the sale of timber to Japan. There are 20,000 sawmills in Japan, supplying housing and furnishings for 120 million people, but U.S. legislation passed in 1968 practically bars them from American markets. It bans exports of unfinished logs cut on federally owned land, which amount to some 65 percent of the softwood saw-timber inventory in the United States, and dictates that all such logs must be processed prior to export. The law even prohibits "substitution," that is, the purchase of federal timber by American merchants who export timber cut on private lands.[10]

Surely, such measures neither reduce the U.S. merchandise trade deficit with Japan nor improve U.S.-Japanese relations. And yet, they continue to spring forth from the primitive notion that the log-export ban forces foreigners to purchase finished products and thereby provides employment to wood processors and furniture makers. Fortunately, political force does not produce sales and employment; both obey only the laws of the market. The timber legislation actually has reduced employment in the American timber industry and prevents employment in cutting and shipping timber to Japan. It serves to reduce the marginal productivity of labor, to lower wage rates in both the United States and Japan and, wherever labor resists the downward pressure, contributes to mass unemployment. It puts the misunderstood interest of a powerful special-interest group ahead of national interest and gives much ammunition to the neo-mercantilists who are fretting about the merchandise trade imbalances.

"Buy American"

There are many more U.S. barriers to trade with Japan and other countries. The most noticeable probably are "Buy American" statutes that give preference to domestic products in Federal and state government contracts. Federal agencies are required to pay up to 6 percent more for products made in the United States. The federal aid program to mass transit systems requires that only American materials be used. The foreign-aid program requires that at least 50 percent of the gross tonnage of all commodities thus financed be carried by American flag vessels. At least 18 states restrict the use of foreign steel and aluminum and order the purchase of domestic products. Many require state bids to carry a clause restricting the use of foreign materials and calling for American-made products. Many local authorities enact building codes that ban the use of foreign materials.

Countless Federal statutes and regulations prevent or limit imports of agricultural products such as beef, dairy produce, mandarin oranges, and sugar. In recent years the U.S. government sought voluntary restraints of foreign sales, which were as voluntary as a judge's temporary restraining order. In recent months it finally dispensed with the pretense of voluntarism. Protection from foreign competition now covers all basic industries that are forced to compete in U.S. markets. Its costs to American consumers in the form of higher goods prices amount to many billions of dollars. A recent study estimated the 1980 costs at more than $58 billion, or $255 per American consumer.[11] They probably have more than doubled since then. Its costs to American workers in the form of lower labor productivity and higher rates of unemployment can only be surmised.

The pressures for protection from foreign competition continue to grow in the United States and other countries. Well-organized groups, especially organized labor, use the political apparatus to reap economic gains through political force. Unable to compete effectively and suffering from depression and unemployment, for which they deny all responsibility, they seek refuge with government and its coercive powers. They noisily demand protection from foreign competition that is held responsible for their plight. Economists do know, however, that mass unemployment, no matter how painful it may be, cannot be placed on the doorsteps of foreigners. It is a self-inflicted evil of radical interventionism that cannot be alleviated by beggar-thy-neighbor policies. Protectionism only exacerbates it.

---

1. Cf. theoretical works: Gottfried Haberler, *The Theory of International Trade* (London: Hodge, [1933] 1936); also his *Survey of International Trade Theory*, Rev. and enl. edition, (Princeton University International Finance Section, [1954] 1961); James E. Meade, *The Theory of International Economic Policy*, Vol. 2; *Trade and Welfare* (New York: Oxford University Press, 1955); Ragnar Nurkse, *Problems of Capital Formation in Underdeveloped Countries* (New York: Oxford University Press, [1953] 1962); Jacob Viner, *Studies in the Theory of International Trade* (New York: Harper & Row, 1937); Leland B. Yeager and David G. Tuerck, *Foreign Trade and U.S. Policy: The Case for Free International Trade* (New York: Praeger Publishers, 1976). See also the classical historical work of Frank W. Taussig, *The Tariff History of the United States* (New York: Putnam, [1888] 1931).

2. See Melvyn B. Krauss, "Ill Fares the Welfare States," *Policy Review* 18 (Fall 1981), pp. 133–138; also *The New Protectionism: The Welfare State and International Trade* (New York: New York University Press, 1978).

3. Robert B. Reich, "Beyond Free Trade," *Foreign Affairs* 61 (Spring 1983), pp. 773–804; Bob Kuttner, "The Free Trade Fallacy," *New Republic*, March 28, 1983, pp. 16–21; G. William Miller, ed., *Regrowing the American Economy* (Englewood Cliffs, N.J.: Prentice-Hall, 1983); Leonard Silk, *The Economists* (New York: Avon Books, 1978); see also *Allied Industrial Worker*, Official Newspaper of the Allied Industrial Workers of America (AFL-CIO) International Union, Milwaukee, Wisc.; September 1984; *CWA News*, Communication Workers of America, AFL-CIO, Washington, D.C., September 1984.

4. See Melvyn B. Krauss, *Development Without Aid* (New York: McGraw-Hill, 1983), especially Chapter 7.

5. Mordechai E. Kreinin, "Wage Competitiveness in the U.S. Auto and Steel Industries," *Contemporary Policy Issues* 4 (January 1984), pp. 39–50.

6. See David Ricardo, *Works and Correspondence*, Edited by Piero Sraffa (Cambridge University Press, 1951–1955), Vol. I, *On the Principles of Political Economy and Taxation*.

7. Council of Economic Advisers, *Annual Report* (Washington, D.C.: Government Printing Office, 1984).

8. Beth deHamel, James R. Ferry, William W. Hogan, and Joseph S. Nie, Jr., *The Export of Alaskan Crude Oil: An Analysis of the Economic and National Security Benefits* (Cambridge, Mass.: Putnam, Hayes, and Bartlett, Inc., 1983).

9. Steve H. Hanke, "U.S.-Japanese Trade: Myth and Realities," *Cato Journal*, 3/3, Winter 1983/84, p. 762.

10. Barney Dowdle and Steve H. Hanke, "Public Timber Policy and the Wood-Products Industry," in M. Bruce Johnson and Robert Deacon, eds., *Forest Lands, Public and Private* (Cambridge, Mass.: Ballinger Publishing Co., 1984).

11. See Murray L. Weidenbaum, *Business, Government and the Public,* 2nd ed. (Englewood Cliffs, N.J.: Prentice-Hall, 1981), pp. 253–255; also "The High Cost of Protectionism," *Cato Journal*, 3/3, Winter 1983/84, pp. 777–791.

Free Trade and the Irish Famine

by John P. Finneran

In the mid-nineteenth century, the political life of Great Britain was torn by a great debate on the principles of protection and free trade. The debate, with its triumph for the free-trade cause, remains equally relevant today, for it shows that protection, whatever its theoretical merits, is ruinous in human terms. The cornerstone of the free-trade victory was the repeal of the corn laws by the Tory government of Sir Robert Peel in 1846.

The Tories and the Corn Laws

The Tory party had had an ambivalent history toward protection and free trade. On the one hand, the Tories under William Pitt the Younger had favored free trade. With the onset of the Napoleonic wars, however, this policy was interrupted. When peace was established, the price of wheat and other grains, with their supply from abroad augmented by the increase in commerce that followed with the peace, went into a steep decline. Heeding the requests of landowners, who constituted the main pillar of Tory support, the Tory government passed the Corn Law of 1815, the first of a series of such laws that effectively excluded foreign grains from the domestic market. (It should be noted that the term "corn" in this context does not refer exclusively to maize, but to grains generally, and to wheat especially.)

When the issue of free trade versus protection came to a head, it would split the Tory party asunder. Indeed, Peel himself reflected his party's dual heritage. At first a strong supporter of protection, Peel became ambiguous, and finally came to favor free trade.

Punch magazine satirized Peel's attempt to bridge both wings of his party by a cartoon which showed him as a rider standing astride two horses at once. *Punch* commented: "The world has been lately astonished by the very rapid act of horsemanship performed by SIR R. PEEL on his two celebrated chargers, Protection and Free Trade. Protection is a very heavy charger, but Free Trade is a light and active filly, always

Mr. Finneran is a writer from Marshfield, Massachusetts. This article originally appeared in the December 1991 issue of *The Freeman*.

going ahead with great speed and energy. The great merit of PEEL consists in the skill he has exhibited in giving the rein, now to one, and now to the other, with wonderful dexterity; now tightening the bridle, and now relaxing it; and, indeed, playing fast and loose with wonderful dexterity. Though he evidently has greater control over Free Trade, he controls Protection with remarkable adroitness. Altogether, his performance is among the most wonderful efforts of modern horsemanship."[1]

In economic terms, the case against protection is simple enough: It benefits the few at the expense of the many. The protected domestic interest benefits from the fact that foreign products are excluded or can only compete at a significant disadvantage. Less competition means the domestic interest can raise the price and lessen the quality of its product, leaving domestic consumers (that is, the vast majority of the population) with the choice of paying more for an inferior product or doing without. In the case of basic food products like grain, of course, this is a Hobson's choice, since everyone must eat.

It is no surprise, then, that the corn laws were from the outset vigorously supported by landowners, who grew domestic grain, and vigorously opposed by non-landowners, who had to pay more for their bread, and by classical liberal theorists. The case against protection had been made eloquently by Adam Smith in *The Wealth of Nations* as far back as 1776, but the depression of 1838 to 1842 caused a new generation of free trade proponents to rise to the fore. An Anti-Corn Law League was founded and expressed its views through meetings, petitions, pamphlets, and speakers. Two great orators, Richard Cobden and John Bright, contributed mightily toward enlisting popular sympathy in the free-trade cause.

It appears that Peel himself was moving in his own mind slowly but inexorably toward support for repeal of the corn laws in the early 1840s. But any lingering resistance he felt toward repeal were swept away decisively by new and calamitous events in Ireland.

The Irish Famine

In August 1845, the potato crop in Ireland failed, beginning the frightful Irish Famine of 1845 to 1848. In the devastating hunger that followed, Ireland's pre-famine population of 8 million was reduced by death and emigration to 6½ million within three years. In addition, in the summer of 1847, 3 million were kept alive solely through charity and public jobs.[2]

A peacetime famine on such a scale had been unseen in Europe for centuries, and with good reason: Improved distribution systems meant that the effects of local crop failures could be mitigated by food brought from afar. Without the perverse effects of protection coupled with a land system that kept the Irish peasants cash poor and therefore unduly dependent for survival on their personal potato crops, the same should have been true for the Irish famine. Indeed, even as Irishmen were starving, Ireland's abundant wheat and maize harvests were being shipped to England. The effect of the corn laws was thus the following: Despite an abundance of food, both in Great Britain and abroad, the artificially high price of grain placed bread beyond the economic reach of cash-poor Irish deprived through the potato crop failure of their major source of income.

When criticized for advancing free-trade measures that overreacted to events in Ireland, Peel exclaimed: "You may think I have taken too great precautions against Irish famine; you are mistaken. Events will prove that the precautions are not unnecessary. But even if it were not so, the motive is to rescue a whole population from the possibility of calamity and disease; and I shall, under these circumstances, be easy under such an accusation."[3]

The Oregon Dispute

A fortunate by-product of Peel's free-trade measures was their effects on relations with the United States. Free trade, in classical liberal theory, is conducive to peace. "Free trade," Richard Cobden asked rhetorically, "What is it? Why, breaking down the barriers that separate nations; those barriers behind which nestle the feelings of pride, revenge, hatred, and jealousy which every now and then break their bonds and deluge whole countries with blood; those feelings which nourish the poison of war and conquest, which assert that without conquest we can have no trade, which foster that lust for conquest and dominion which sends forth your warrior chiefs to sanction devastation through other lands."[4]

In the case of the Oregon dispute of the 1840s, the theory conformed with reality. America and Great Britain at this time stood on the brink of war over ownership of the Oregon Territory (the present-day states of Oregon and Washington and part of the Canadian province of British Columbia). James K. Polk had been elected to the White House in 1844 under the slogan "54 40' or Fight!"—a claim to the entire Oregon Territory for the United States. While it would be an exaggeration to state that Peel's free-trade policy of this time was the sole factor that averted war (certainly America's simultaneous dispute with Mexico, which would ultimately degenerate into the Mexican War, was at least as important in causing the U.S. to seek a compromise), Peel's policies *did*, at least, contribute toward creating an atmosphere that was more conducive to a peaceful resolution of the conflict.

Hence *Punch* wrote: "The English Premier has taken the happiest method of dealing with the American President. POLK fires off inflammatory messages, while PEEL returns the attack with Free-Trade measures. The latter will, we have every hope, prove irresistible, and POLK will not be able to make a successful stand against the very felicitous mode of warfare adopted by our Free-Trade Minister. It is not likely that the American people will be misguided enough to continue a hostility, which will be so directly opposed to their own interests. . . . America may, if it pleases, pelt us with its corn, while we return the compliment by pitching into the United States some of our manufactured articles. This will be much better for both parties than an exchange of lead, whether in the form of swan or grape, or packed in canister."[5]

The End of the Peel Ministry

Once he had decided on repeal of the corn laws, Peel had to convince a parliamentary majority—which proved to be no easy task. In December 1845, Peel tried to effect emergency reductions in tariffs through orders in council, executive orders requiring a cabinet majority but no parliamentary vote, but failed to gain a majority in his own cabinet and was forced to resign. The Whig leader, Lord John Russell, was unable to form a cabinet, and Queen Victoria had to call Peel back. Peel was able to form a new ministry with the addition of William Gladstone, the future Liberal prime minister, as colonial secretary.

The new Peel ministry's attempts to repeal the corn laws were met in the Tory party with vigorous opposition led by Gladstone's future nemesis, Benjamin Disraeli, until then a little-known member of Parliament. Finally, after a great deal of agitation, on June 25, 1846, the corn laws were repealed with the support of Whig and Irish members of Parliament.[6] But the old Tory party was irreparably split. Indeed, on the very night that the corn laws were repealed, Peel's government lost a vote of confidence on its larger Irish policy, and Peel's political life came to an end. Only four years later, in 1850, he died following an accident suffered while riding a horse through Green Park.

Winston Churchill summed up Peel's career as follows: "He was not a man of broad and ranging modes of thought, but he understood better than any of his contemporaries the needs of the country, and he had the outstanding courage to change his views in order to meet them.

It is true that he split his party, but there are greater crimes than that."[7]

Peel's own epitaph of his political career, delivered the night of his government's fall, deserves to be quoted at length: "I shall, I fear, leave office with a name severely censured by many honorable men who, on public principle, deeply regret the severance of party ties—who deeply regret that severance, not from any interested or personal motives, but because they believe fidelity to party, the existence of a great party, and the maintenance of a great party, to be powerful instruments of good government. I shall surrender power, severely censured, I fear, by many honorable men, who, from no interested motives, have adhered to the principles of protection, because they looked upon them as important to the welfare and interests of the country. I shall leave a name execrated, I know, by every monopolist [Peel's speech, reports *Punch*, was here interrupted by "Loud cheers and laughter"] who, professing honorable opinions, would maintain protection for his own benefit. But it may be that I shall sometimes be remembered with expressions of goodwill, in those places which are the abodes of men whose lot it is to labor and earn their daily bread by the sweat of their brow; in such places, perhaps, my name may be remembered with expressions of goodwill, when they who inhabit them recruit their exhausted strength with abundant and untaxed food, the sweeter because no longer leavened with a sense of injustice."[8]

---

1. *Punch*, vol. 10, January 1846–June 1846, p. 104.

2. Figures from Edmund Curtis, *A History of Ireland* (London: Methuen & Co., 1968), p. 368.

3. *Punch*, "Introduction" to vol. 10, p. 3.

4. Richard Cobden, *Speeches on Questions of Public Policy*, vol. I (London, 1870), p. 79, cited in Michael Howard, *War and the Liberal Conscience* (New Brunswick, N.J.: Rutgers University Press, 1986), pp. 42–43.

5. *Punch*, p. 155.

6. Technically, the corn laws were not repealed at this date. Maize was allowed to enter tariff free, and tariffs for other grains were drastically reduced (the duty on wheat, for example, was reduced to one-fourth of its previous level). The bill passed at this time scheduled an abolition of grain tariffs (except for a "mere nominal duty . . . for the purpose of procuring statistical returns of the quantity imported") for February 1849. An amendment to repeal the corn laws outright was defeated by a margin of 187 votes. See *Punch*, "Introduction," pp. 2–3.

7. Winston Churchill, *The Great Democracies* (New York: Dodd, Mead, and Co., 1965), p. 62.

8. *Punch*, "Introduction," p. 3.

Environment and Free Trade

by Jo Kwong

Environmental activists, who typically take a unified stance on major issues ranging from global warming to endangered species protection, experienced an unusual split with regard to the North American Free Trade Agreement (NAFTA). Generally speaking, environmentalists divided between those who were convinced that free trade would lead to greater damage to the environment, and those who believed that freer trade would stimulate national economies, ultimately creating more resources to help protect the environment.

NAFTA brought these two positions into stark conflict. Most vocal was the anti-NAFTA environmental lobby. The Sierra Club, Friends of the Earth, and Public Citizen, among others, argued that NAFTA would provide an opportunity for U.S. companies to migrate to Mexico and escape more rigid American environmental laws. Larry Williams, international program director for the Sierra Club, cautioned that the flight of factories from the United States to Mexico: "would increase pollution loading levels on the continent and would trigger pressures within the United States to lower environmental standards to improve competitiveness in order to stop the flights."[1]

This thinking, however, is flawed on several counts. First, there is little historical evidence of polluting industries migrating to countries where environmental standards are lax. While many developing countries are experiencing rapid industrial growth, this reflects the economic stage that they are going through, rather than environmentally induced migration. Polluting industries, that spend heavily on controls, remain concentrated in the developed countries. Ironically, it was the closed, protectionist countries—particularly in the former Communist world—that became pollution havens.

Environmental regulations pose a negligible factor on migration decisions because they typically comprise less than 4 to 5 percent of total costs. Other factors may easily overwhelm such a modest cost savings: On my last trip to Mexico City, several people indicated that prob-

Dr. Jo Kwong is Director of Environmental Programs with the Atlas Economic Research Foundation in Fairfax, Virginia. This article was originally published in the February 1994 issue of *The Freeman*.

lems like unstable telephone service are of far greater concern than environmental considerations in making location decisions.

Moreover, irrespective of the level of regulation, companies are fearful of liability arising from environmental accidents. A firm's desire to protect its reputation in its home market weakens the temptation to cut environmental costs—companies are sensitive to the demands of "green" consumers in export markets.

Another common environmentalist objection to reducing trade barriers is that doing so will inhibit harmonization of environmental, health, and safety standards regarding production processes. For example, in a highly publicized case involving yellowfin tuna imports, environmental activists ran newspaper advertisements with the headline "SABOTAGE! of America's Health, Food Safety and Environmental Laws." The ads argued that "the only thing free about free trade is the freedom it gives the world's largest corporations to circumvent democracy and kill those 'pesky' laws that protect people and the planet." The activists were furious about a GATT ruling against a U.S. ban on tuna imports from Mexico, imposed because the United States alleged that Mexican fishing boats kill too many dolphins. Yet, according to the *Journal of Commerce,* the U.S. killing rate was significantly greater than that of Mexico: "In 1988 the US fleet caught 70,000 tons of yellowfin tuna and killed 19,000 dolphins; in 1990 the Mexican fleet caught 120,000 tons of yellowfin tuna and killed only 16,000 dolphins."[2] Thus, this controversy provides a better example of economic protectionism than environmental destruction.

Other allegations by the U.S. environmental lobby illustrate how politics has overtaken science in the making of domestic law. Activists warn, for example, that foreign nations might use pesticides that are banned in the United States. Therefore, trade restrictions are necessary. However, the United States greatly overregulates most pesticides: many are banned even if the residues found in food are minuscule and threat to human health is virtually nonexistent. Much of this is a result of the Delaney Clause, a provision of federal food safety law, which states that "no additive shall be deemed to be safe if it is found to induce cancer when ingested by man or animal." Much has changed since the clause was added in 1958, particularly the ability to detect minute chemical residues measured in parts per million, even parts per billion. Thus, the law now bans all sorts of products that would have been considered perfectly safe in 1958.

Such draconian rules are inefficient in America; in poorer, Third World nations they could prove to be downright fatal. DDT is a case in point. U.S. environmental activists, not satisfied with banning the substance in America, are still trying to ban it elsewhere around the world. To this day, serious controversy persists about whether DDT really poses a serious environmental danger. The World Health Organization, the U.S. Surgeon General, and the National Science Foundation have been unable to document many of the charges raised against DDT over the decades.

In contrast, the harm to human health from the ban on DDT has been very real. In just two decades of DDT use, malaria deaths in India were cut by 98 percent, raising the average life span by 18 years. In the nearly 20 years since the ban, malaria death rates have soared. Similar trends have been observed in Sri Lanka, Bangladesh, Burma, and Thailand. Thus, the environmental benefits of the DDT ban may have been far outweighed by the human costs.[3]

As this case suggests, many environmentalist arguments against trade reflect more emotion than rational analysis. In fact, with freer trade it is probable that Mexican ecological, health, and safety standards would evolve towards U.S. standards, rather than vice versa. One reason is that most international companies have universal policies in place regardless of where they are operating. They don't set lower standards for operations in less developed countries. In this way Mexico's environment would be enhanced by opening up trade.

Furthermore, companies typically expect rising environmental standards in developing-country markets, so they tend to introduce state-of-the-art technology initially. One GATT report published early last year cited cases in which firms gain a competitive edge by investing first in clean technologies.

A Conflict of Visions

If the environmental arguments against freer trade are so flawed, why are they nevertheless held so tenaciously? One reason is the intellectual framework of many environmental activists. Broadening trade runs against the environmental vision, particularly that of local self-reliance and a return to a simpler, low-technology world. Consider the argument of David Morris of the Institute for Local Self-Reliance: "Most people believe that a global economy is the only path to a higher standard of living as well as the inevitable next step in economic evolution. The economic emphasis on imports and exports continues to guide our thinking even when we can see that it endangers the survival of humans and other species."

In his view, the "key to achieving a Green future . . . is localizing the world economy."[4] The problem with this quaint way of thinking is that it ignores elementary economic concepts. For instance, as long as trade is voluntary, both partners benefit; otherwise they wouldn't trade. The buyer of a shirt, for example, values the shirt more than the money spent, while the seller values the money more. Trade makes the world economy more efficient by allowing nations to capitalize on their strengths.

Of course, Morris accepts trade within his local region, but where does he draw his trade boundary lines? If it makes sense for Morris' butcher and baker to trade in their region, how about trading with the community next door? Morris' vision makes no rational sense, but retains enormous emotional appeal.

Another point that should interest environmentalists is the fact that opening economies to the competitive global marketplace forces nations to become more efficient and waste fewer resources. For instance, in the Soviet Union every barrel of crude oil consumed produces $253 of GNP; the corresponding outputs for the United States, western Germany, and Japan are $341, $420, and $639, respectively. Similarly, Swedish sawmills use 98 percent of a tree in timber production whereas Malaysian mills use only 40 percent. The sort of waste and inefficiency evident in more closed economies is responsible for much of the environmental degradation of the world today. Competition, which forces technological improvements and the modernization of plants and equipment, can vastly enhance environmental quality.

Freer trade would boost environmental amenities in other ways. For instance, much of the current pollution on the U.S. side of the border results from crowding on the other side, largely as a result of the *maquiladora* program. That program gives special tariff treatment to Mexican industries that import U.S. products for assembly and re-export. It originally required Mexican firms to locate along the border in order to receive the program's benefits. While these restrictions have been eased, others remain which encourage firms to remain in the border area. Free trade would reduce today's artificial incentive for border crowding.

The bulk of the environmental improvements are most likely to occur in Mexico. Companies operating in developing countries bring new technologies to market and, for reasons mentioned earlier, are likely to adhere to American standards. In addition, Mexican companies would find they have to adhere to standards acceptable to U.S. consumers in order to successfully export. Just the promise of free trade is already encouraging U.S.-Mexico cooperation on the cleanup of their common boundary. Before NAFTA, U.S. activists largely ignored environmental problems in Mexico. Now, the two countries are hammering out details on the Border Plan, the most comprehensive attempt to cooperate on cleanup.

Perhaps the biggest reason for environmental gains in Mexico from freer trade, however, would result from increased economic prosperity. To some environmentalists, this seems backwards. Many argue against trade because it encourages industrialization, which in turn, is blamed for pollution. Yet the experience of Western developed countries is just the opposite. Over the long term, emissions eventually fall, even as economic growth continues to increase. Several years ago, Hoover research fellow Mikhail Bernstam detailed what he calls "the environmental split of the 1970s and 1980s"—a divergence between consumption and pollution involving Western market economies and the socialist world. He found that resource use and discharges began to decline rapidly in those nations with competitive markets, even as economic growth continued. In contrast, during the same two decades, consumption and environmental disruption were rapidly increasing in the USSR and European socialist countries even though their economies slowed down and eventually stagnated.[5]

Bernstam's conclusions are borne out by other studies as well. Gene Grossman and Ann Krueger examined air quality in urban areas of the developed and developing world. Their analysis related the level of pollutants to the level of the nation's per capita GDP. They found that concentrations of sulfur dioxide have risen with incomes at low levels of per capita income; fallen at higher levels of per capita income; and leveled off when per capita income reached about $5,000 (1988 U.S. dollars).

The basic point is that countries must be rich before they can be clean. As societies become wealthier, they attach a greater value to environmental quality. Ecological prosperity is a luxury that only developed nations can afford. Trade enables countries to become richer, and, as the studies suggest, this in turn reduces pollution.

Free-Market Environmentalism

Another interesting finding of the Bernstam study was that the strictness of government environmental regulation does not correlate with the drop in pollution. If anything, he writes, there is a slight *negative* correlation. Far more important in determining emission levels is an economy's incentive structure. Thus, as we discuss markets and trade within North America, we should consider using markets in natural resources to foster incentives for environmental stewardship.

Free-market environmentalism is premised on the idea that the failure to apply markets has led to many of today's environmental problems. Air, water, and land pollution are often the worst on common property resources such as those owned by the government. In these cases, no one is responsible for seeing that resources are used efficiently and adequately protected.

This is the essence of the standard textbook concept called the "tragedy of the commons," whereby users of communal land will use the property as intensively as possible, since they gain little benefit from conserving the resource. Users of communal grazing lands face the incentive to boost personal gains by overgrazing the land at public expense. In contrast, users of private land face the incentive to consider the costs of maintaining the pasture at varying intensities of grazing. Of course, many people object that the owners will exploit the land for profit, caring little about environmental preservation. However, property rights give even an uncaring owner a financial incentive to preserve his land, since overgrazing will lead to both economic ruin and environmental devastation. By maintaining the property, he maximizes both.

Unfortunately, the standard approach to environmental problems in the United States has been regulatory rather than market-oriented. But most major environmental initiatives, such as Superfund, the Endangered Species Act, and the Federal Water Pollution Control Act, have fallen far short of their goals. Most have been extremely expensive and relatively ineffective. Some have even created severe disincentives for people to preserve the environment. Consider the Endangered Species Act, intended to protect plants and animals that are experiencing serious population declines. Under the act, it is a federal crime to use land in a way that endangers the habitat of protected plants and animals. Once an endangered species shows up on private property, the landowner is no longer free to use the land without federal approval. Some owners have lost millions of dollars after the discovery of protected wildlife on their property. As a result, many now discourage natural habitat and destroy any protected species that they find—the "shoot, shovel, and shut-up" strategy.

Such problems are no stranger to Mexico. As Roberto Salinas, Executive Director of the Centro de Investigaciones Sobre la Libre Empresa in Mexico City, writes, "the lack of property titles in rural farming areas has forced peasants to turn to burning the rich forests in southern Mexico in search of new arable land." As Mexico confronts its many environmental problems, hopefully its leaders will consider more efficient market-oriented conservation strategies. They are more likely to do so as part of a freer economic and trade regime.

Summary

In the end, anti-free trade environmentalists need to address the evidence and, equally important, rethink their warped vision of the future, a "shallow ecology" that, intentionally or not, aims at protecting the health and affluence of people in the developed countries. Argues Roberto Sanchez, an environmental specialist at the Colegio de la Frontera Norte, a research institute in Tijuana, environmental changes will only occur "if the American environmentalists give up some of their romantic notions and let [Mexico] find its own way." Environmentalists may "want to save the planet, but it is not the same planet on their side of the border as it is on [Mexico's]. They can afford to defend the environment for its own sake. Our people must use the environment to survive."[6]

Trade negotiations, including but not limited to NAFTA, present unique opportunities to coordinate trade with environmental policy. The evidence is overwhelming that opening markets will provide both economic and environmental prosperity for all parties. It is the poverty of a closed economy, not free trade, that threatens ecological degradation around the globe.

Moreover, free-market environmentalism provides a means for advancing both economic and ecological ends. It uses rather than suppresses the powerful incentives embodied in property rights and voluntary trade to better protect environmental and natural resources. As environmental concerns grow in importance in the global economy, so too will debate over this alternative vision.

---

1. Larry Williams, "Mexican Trade Deal: Fallout or Fantasy?" *The Washington Times*, December 22, 1991.

2. *Journal of Commerce*, October 28, 1991, p. 5a; November 5, 1991, p. 8A.

3. Warren Brookes, "An Economic Silent Spring," *The Detroit News*, March 11, 1990.

4. David Morris, "The materials we need to create a sustainable society lie close to home," *The Utne Reader*, November/December 1989, p. 84.

5. Mikhail S. Bernstam, "The Wealth of Nations and the Environment," Institute of Economic Affairs, London, 1991.

6. Quoted in Fred Smith, "Environmental Quality, Economic Growth, and Trade," paper presented at the Cato Conference, "Liberty in the Americas, Free Trade and Beyond," Mexico City, May 19–22, 1992.

A Closer Look at "Dumping"

by S.J. Cicero

One hears frequent complaints that foreigners, particularly the Japanese, "dump" their merchandise (sell it below cost) in American markets, thus making it difficult for U.S. manufacturers to compete. Is there any truth to these charges?

First, we need to bear in mind that there is generally no such thing as a single "cost"; costs can be calculated in several ways. There are average costs over various lengths of time, overhead costs that can be amortized by a number of techniques, quantity-related variations, and so on. When items are being mass-produced, the "cost" of a specific finished product depends on operating costs, which are bound to fluctuate. Additionally, what about the cost of failing to sell the item in a timely fashion—the "opportunity cost" of manufacturing one kind of item instead of another?

There are many reasons for selling merchandise at or below "cost." One of the most common is the attempt to secure a greater market share. Furthermore, a foreign market may be much larger than the home market, giving rise to economies of scale for goods shipped abroad which do not apply in the home market, so that even such price differentials as these are not sure signs of predatory intent.

Second, the sole purpose of production is consumption. This means that goods not consumed are wasted, and represent a loss of profit opportunity. In a competitive market, this prompts each manufacturer to concentrate on what he does best, and to continually improve his production techniques to hold the competition at bay. Profit is the essential link that drives this process. The profit incentive encourages innovation, and reinvested profits enable innovations to be brought on-line. To operate deliberately at a loss is a risky strategy that, in the absence of government "assistance," can be kept up only for a short time.

Third, while it is true that a country's government may subsidize a favored industry, enabling that industry to outdo its rivals, this can be done only at the expense of other industries, rendering them less com-

---

Mr. Cicero, a computer software engineer, resides in Arleta, California. This article was originally published in the June 1991 issue of *The Freeman*.

petitive. The net effect is to reduce overall productivity, putting the country as a whole at a competitive disadvantage.

This is so because the taxation required to shift capital to the favored industry tends to reduce incentives in both the favored and the taxed sectors. In addition, the act of collecting and distributing the tax is costly, with no offsetting increase in production. When the state diverts resources to its favored industries, the whole economy is rendered less efficient.

Fourth, the "dumping" of goods into the American market benefits U.S. consumers, who enjoy lower prices and thus increased purchasing power. The particular industry that competes with the cost-cutter does, of course, face a challenge. But rather than calling for tariffs and import quotas, a better strategy would be for the threatened company to cut overhead where possible, shift production to more profitable lines, and emphasize quality and/or promote product differences when advertising. Given this, an industry which is still uncompetitive will contract in favor of its rival, freeing up workers and capital for more profitable and therefore more productive endeavors.

If U.S. industries can't compete, it is largely due to misguided policies, both within the industries themselves and inflicted upon them by our own government. Before we blame Japan or Germany for our troubles, we would do well to get our own house in order. Taxation and inflation hurt our ability to compete, as do burdensome regulations. Pro-union legislation, pitting labor against management and nonunion workers, drives up costs. Tariffs and import quotas, which enable a company to continue operating in an inefficient manner, hurt overall productivity and thus harm consumers. In the case of Japan, we are foolish to accuse the Japanese government of subsidizing their industries, when we subsidize virtually all of Japan's defense, thus freeing much of their tax revenue for use in subsidies.

Economic principles are always the same, whether we consider trade across national boundaries, state borders—or across the street. People benefit from unrestricted trade. Attempts to restrain trade always reduce overall prosperity, particularly for consumers who would otherwise find the imported goods less expensive. It would be helpful if we could remember that the Japanese people trade with the American people, to the mutual benefit of both. We are partners in trade with the Japanese, not adversaries.

I'm All for Free Trade, But . . .

by Mark Skousen

"The dogma [of free trade] does not stand up. . . . Import relief
in the 1980s saved America's industrial base—and countless
jobs—at tiny cost."
>—Pat Buchanan, "How the Rust Belt was Revived,"
>*Washington Times*, July 20, 1994

Conservative columnist and political commentator Pat Buchanan
needs to take a refresher course in Econ 101. He cites a study by economist Alan Tonelson in *Foreign Affairs* magazine (July/August 1994)
supporting his "America First" doctrine of economic protectionism.
"The United States ought not to surrender any weapon in its arsenal of
defense for vital U.S. economic interests," says Buchanan.

Tonelson concurs: "Five major American industries—automotive,
steel, machine tool, semiconductor, and textile—received significant
relief from imports through intelligently structured trade laws. Those
industries have confounded the predictions of laissez-faire economic
ideologies by gaining market share at home and in some cases abroad,
contributing to job creation and reinvigorating American competitiveness."

Thus, after Tokyo agreed to voluntary import limits in 1981, American automakers achieved an astonishing comeback. The Big Three
came out with new products such as the minivan and compact utility
vehicles. Investment in new plant and equipment resulted in a substantial increase in productivity and quality of U.S. cars.

After Reagan negotiated bilateral agreements limiting imports of
finished steel in 1984, investment and worker productivity in the U.S.
steel industry soared, making the United States one of the lowest-cost
producers in the world. Import curbs on machine tools, semiconduc-
tors, and textiles saw similar results—increased research and develop-

---

Dr. Skousen teaches in the Department of Economics at Rollins College in Winter
Park, Florida. He serves as editor of *Forecasts and Strategies,* one of the largest investment
newsletters in the country. This article was originally published in the October 1994 issue
of *The Freeman.*

ment, investment, cost-cutting, job creation, and retooling. The United States improved its competitiveness in all these markets.

Buchanan concludes: "The conventional wisdom was wrong."

Is This the Whole Story?

Before we reject two centuries of sound economic wisdom, let us consider all the relevant factors. Messrs. Buchanan and Tonelson conveniently forget to mention the environment in which these five industries performed so well. The reality is that virtually all industrial groups expanded sharply during the "Seven Fat Years" of the Reagan era, as Robert Bartley calls it. The free-trade critics have committed the classic *post hoc, ergo propter hoc* argument. Just because an event (import restrictions) occurs simultaneously to another event (economic recovery) does not mean that one is the primary cause of the other. There may be other, more powerful forces at work. Indeed, in the midst of a sharp recession (1981), Congress cut tax rates substantially for individuals, corporations, and investors, thus stimulating a "supply-side" revolution. Furthermore, in the summer of 1982, the Federal Reserve reversed its tight-money, high-interest-rate policy in favor of easy money and lower interest rates. The low-interest rate, tax-cutting era continued almost throughout the 1980s, factors which most likely dwarfed the impact of import restrictions.

One should also not ignore the impact of a falling dollar since 1985 on the improvement in U.S. exports and foreign competition.

In short, the Rust Belt was revived primarily because of the "supply-side" revolution of tax cuts, deregulation, and an accommodating monetary policy—not protectionism. At least Messrs. Buchanan and Tonelson provide little evidence that the protected industries outperformed all other industries.

Global Trade Is Inevitable

This is not to say that U.S. producers didn't benefit from import relief. Undoubtedly, they did benefit. After all, tariffs and quotas aren't the measles. Yet the benefits may not have been all that great. The auto, steel, and textile industries would probably have done almost as well without the import restrictions.

Even before the import quotas were imposed in the 1980s, most of the leaders in these industries had recognized that the world was rapidly moving toward global free trade. Ford, for example, had already decided to take the Japanese and the Germans head-on in building high-tech automobiles. Gradually more and more of the components of "American" products are made in foreign countries. Despite all kinds of restrictions and regulations in the textile and apparel industries, more and more shoes and clothing are being made in Asia and Latin America—by American-based companies. Global free trade is a simple fact of life and any manufacturer in the United States who doesn't recognize its inevitability is headed straight for bankruptcy court.

Cost-Benefit Analysis

In his great book *Economics in One Lesson*, Henry Hazlitt says that a good economist looks at how a policy affects all groups, not just one group. His story of the broken window is a classic.

We need to apply his "one lesson" to the free-trade debate. Yes, import relief helps the 21 highly protected sectors of the U.S. economy. It maintains thousands of American jobs in these industries. It keeps prices and wages higher than what they would be.

But what about the other groups in the economy—are they helped or hurt by import restrictions? According to the latest study by the Institute for International Economics, American consumers paid $70 billion more for goods and services as a direct result of import protection in 1990. Now, in a $6 trillion economy, that may not seem like much. And, in fact, it demonstrates the high degree of free trade which already exists in the United States.

Nevertheless, the consumer cost per job saved averages about $170,000. Economists Hufbauer and Elliott conclude: "This is far higher than the average annual wage in the protected industries and far more than any current or proposed labor adjustment program would cost."[1]

Tariffs and quotas affect the U.S. economy in many obscure, subtle ways. For example, the voluntary import quotas on Japan resulted in a substantial increase in the importing of higher-priced, larger Japanese cars. Import limits on finished steel forced U.S. automobile companies to pay higher prices on their inputs.

Clearly, most producers benefit from tariffs and quotas, while consumers are hurt. Why don't consumers complain more loudly? Probably because of the nature of the political system. As public-choice economists demonstrate, industry and labor are much better lobbyists than consumers. Moreover, consumers are also producers and may work in protected industries as well. The protectionist story is the same everywhere, in the United States, Japan, or Germany. Everyone favors promoting exports, but not imports.

A Better Idea

While the debate over protectionism rages on, economists and journalists should consider a far better alternative to import relief—tax and regulatory relief for domestic business. One of the primary reasons the auto, steel, and textile industries have had difficulty competing in the world economy is because they lack the capital investment to adopt the latest technology and rebuild their markets. Imagine the impact on American industry if the corporate income tax and the capital gains tax were eliminated? If red tape and regulations were streamlined? Economic growth would be so rapid that we wouldn't even think twice about the need for "import relief" and "fair trade."

---

1. Gary Clyde Hufbauer and Kimberly Ann Elliott, *Measuring the Costs of Protection in the United States* (Washington, D.C.: Institute for International Economics, 1994), back cover.

Index

About the Publisher

The Foundation for Economic Education, Inc., was established in 1946 by Leonard E. Read to study and advance the moral and intellectual rationale for a free society.

The Foundation publishes *The Freeman*, an award-winning monthly journal of ideas in the fields of economics, history, and moral philosophy. FEE also publishes books, conducts seminars, and sponsors a network of discussion clubs to improve understanding of the principles of a free and prosperous society.

FEE is a non-political, non-profit 501(c)(3) tax-exempt organization, supported solely by private contributions and sales of its literature.

For further information, please contact: The Foundation for Economic Education, Inc., 30 South Broadway, Irvington-on-Hudson, New York 10533. Telephone: (914) 591-7230; fax: (914) 591-8910; E-mail: freeman@westnet.com.

If You Liked This Book, You'll Like The Freeman

The Freeman is the source of most of the chapters in this book. Since 1956, it has been published monthly by The Foundation for Economic Education (FEE).

The Freeman offers serious readers a unique source of free-market information. No other magazine, newspaper, or scholarly journal introduces readers to so many implications of what the free society is all about: its moral legitimacy, its tremendous efficiency, and its liberating effects in every area of life.

When FEE began publishing *The Freeman*, there was literally no other source of such popularly written information on the free society. Today, dozens of institutions produce thousands of pages of material every year on the topic.

Despite all the competition (and imitation!), *The Freeman* remains the most effective introduction to the fundamentals of the free society. For newcomers and old-timers, for high school students and Ph.D.'s, *The Freeman* offers new insights of significant value each month.

Why should you read *The Freeman*? Because the world is still in the midst of a monumental battle of ideas. The collapse of European Communism in 1989 has only changed the terms of the debate. It has not changed the fundamental issues.

What are these issues? Government compulsion vs. private choice, collective responsibility vs. personal responsibility, the wisdom of central planners vs. the managerial skills of profit-seeking entrepreneurs, compulsory wealth redistribution vs. voluntary charity, Social Security vs. personal thrift.

All over the world, the debate rages. Yet most people don't know where to begin to sort out fact from fiction.

Do you agree? Then you ought to be reading *The Freeman* every month. Find out for yourself. For a free trial subscription, call (914) 591-7230. Or write to FEE, Irvington-on-Hudson, NY 10533. Do it now.